WOMAN OF VALOR

WOMAN OF VALOR

A STORY OF RESISTANCE, LEADERSHIP & COURAGE

MARTY BROUNSTEIN

Cover Design & Typesetting: Gary A. Rosenberg
Cover art and maps on pages xii and xiiii by Yaki Margulies
Editor: Erica Shur
Photographs reprinted courtesy of Krzysztof Czubaszek, Rosalie Gluckman,
 and Shain Fishman

Square One Publishers
115 Herricks Road
Garden City Park, NY 11040
(516) 535-2010 • (877) 900-BOOK
www.squareonepublishers.com

Library of Congress Cataloging-in-Publication Data

Names: Brounstein, Marty, author.
Title: Woman of valor : a story of resistance leadership & courage / Marty
 Brounstein.
Other titles: Story of resistance leadership & courage
Description: Garden City Park, NY : Square One Publishers, [2021] |
 Includes bibliographical references. | Summary: "A tale of one Jewish
 woman's fight against the Nazis in Poland"--Provided by publisher.
Identifiers: LCCN 2020027104 (print) | LCCN 2020027105 (ebook) | ISBN
 9780757005039 (paperback) | ISBN 9780757055034 (ebook)
Subjects: LCSH: Wrobel, Eta. | Jews--Poland--Łuków (Lublin)--Biography. |
 World War, 1939-1945--Jewish resistance--Poland. | Holocaust, Jewish
 (1939-1945)--Poland--Biography. | Holocaust survivors--United
 States--Biography.
Classification: LCC DS134.72.W76 B76 2020 (print) | LCC DS134.72.W76
 (ebook) | DDC 940.53/18092 [B]--dc23
LC record available at https://lccn.loc.gov/2020027104
LC ebook record available at https://lccn.loc.gov/2020027105

Printed in the United States of America

10   9   8   7   6   5   4   3   2   1

Contents

I have been fortunate in my life to have role models of positive, strong women who have been women of valor in my life.

To Talia Goldenberg

My cousin and the daughter of my first cousin Jeff Goldenberg and Naomi Kirtner; while her life ended way too soon and tragically in her 20's, in the time she was here, her spirit and energy, despite physical health issues, left an indelible and positive impact for me and so many others.

To Goldie Brounstein

The first woman of valor in my life was also the greatest mother one could ever have, and while breast cancer took her too soon before the age of 60, her grace and courage through this illness and her leadership and assertiveness in the way she carried out her life is why you will see her gravestone with the heading of "Woman of Valor" on it.

To Leah Brounstein Baars

I have been a very lucky person to have a most loving and caring wife who has supported me on my journey of many years of sharing these inspirational stories of resistance and rescue in the Holocaust and who has been by my side through difficult times to care and keep me well.

Acknowledgments

Putting this book together was like a journey in seeking the pieces of a jigsaw puzzle. I could not have pulled this together without the support of the Wrobel family. The journey began with Barak Wrobel, one of the grandsons of Eta Chait (Wrobel). He helped connect me to Eta's three children who not only supported me in pulling this story together about their mother but really gave me a true flavor of who this remarkable woman was.

Eta's three children who were instrumental for me are her oldest, Hal Wrobel, her middle child and oldest daughter Shain Fishman, and Ana Wrobel, Barak's mother. Hal gave me good insight into Eta's experience and character, Shain became the source of most of the pictures in this book and really relayed the spirit of her mother. Ana, the retired history teacher, who most talked to her mother over the years about her resistance experience became my point person to bounce questions and thoughts off of throughout my efforts of putting this story together. I am eternally grateful to now call this family, friends of mine.

As the journey and uncovering of the story built, I was able to get help and meet the four children of Chaim Grinbaum, one of Eta's fellow partisans. They all live in the New York City area and were happy to contribute. Thank you to Rosalie Gluckman, Florence Lambert, Jay Grinbaum, and Harry Grinbaum. In addition, the two sons of Jack (Yidl) Woland, Herb and Michael Woland, provided insights about their father, another of Eta's fellow partisans. Thank you to Dr. Shirl Kelemer the daughter of another partisan, David Rendel, for sharing with me about her father.

Furthermore I got help directly from Poland, the central location of the story. A thank you to Kasia Laziuk, who late in life became a friend of the Wrobel family, for her insights and her recognition of the importance of Holocaust education. A major source from Poland was Krzyszt of Czubaszek. He told me to call him Kris, in his perfect English, when we spoke a few times. In his day job, he is a city administrator for the city of Warsaw but his true passion is as a Ph.D. historian. He went and discovered the town of Lukow, where he grew up, actually had a Jewish history to it. His insights about this history and about what was happening in this area during World War II were invaluable.

As I drafted the manuscript I was able to turn to two trusted sources who helped me in shaping it, Dave Roberts and Jodie Russi. They are two master teachers, now retired, but also fine writers. They have been great supporters of mine on my journey over the years of sharing inspirational stories of resistance and rescue in the Holocaust. Then, Mary Ellen Walsh, a freelance editor, came into the picture and guided me in the enhancement of the manuscript, strengthening its storytelling flavor. What was great about Mary Ellen is from the start she loved the character of Eta, so I knew I had the right person to help me.

A special thanks to my nephew Yaki Margulies, whose talents helped in the design of the book cover and the creation of the Poland maps. Great having your ready support for this project.

Of course, none of this happens without the publisher willing to support me in producing these books. This is my second story of resistance and rescue in the Holocaust with Square One Publishers. A big thanks to Rudy Shur, Publisher, and his staff for helping me get this story out. Rudy gave me a wonderful in-house editor who knew how to polish the story while maintaining its flow. A big thanks to editor, Erica Shur.

Preface

Sometimes you are reminded of the importance of your work when you least expect it. I was on travels outside the United States and had a chance to visit a Jewish historical and cultural museum in a beautiful city. (Names and places left out to protect the innocent.) The second floor of this museum is all dedicated to the Holocaust and was the most crowded of the museum's three floors the day I visited, especially with school groups being given guided tours. How much in this whole floor was dedicated to providing information about resistance and rescue in the Holocaust? Next to nothing. At best, a sentence or two about the Jewish revolt known as the Warsaw Ghetto Uprising. As I stood near this little piece, in front of me was one of these school groups led by a museum docent who told the students there was not much Jewish resistance in the Holocaust outside of the Warsaw Ghetto uprising. I was tempted to scream at this false and ignorant statement by the docent, who most likely had no malicious intent behind what he was saying. But this was a reminder of how important it is that the stories of the Jews and non-Jews who stood up against Nazi tyranny during the Holocaust be told, work I have been doing for some years.

Yes, there were Jews who rescued Jews and Jews who fought in resistance units in the many countries of Europe that fell under the occupation of Nazi Germany during World War II. A young Jewish woman at the time named Eta Chait is one of these amazing stories of resistance and rescue.

In fact, one such organization that works to highlight and provide education about Jewish resistance in the Holocaust is the Jewish Partisan Educational Foundation (JPEF) headquartered in San Francisco, California. A few years ago I got to meet the organization's Executive Director, Mitch Braff, who connected me to one of JPEF's board members, Barak Wrobel. Barak is the grandson of Eta Chait. His grandmother, Eta, was a big part of his life growing up in New York. When I first met Barak and wondered if his family would support the idea of me potentially writing a book about his grandmother's resistance experience, he thought this would be the case. He expressed that his mother Anna Wrobel, Aunt Shain Fishman, and Uncle Hal Wrobel—Eta's three children—would most likely be interested in having Eta's resistance story be told to a wider audience and would be supportive in the effort to do so. That proved to be very true.

A Brief Explanation on Names

This remarkable story takes place in Poland. The main person of this story is Eta Chait. Later, Eta's married name was Wrobel. She grew up in the town of Lukow, Poland, where much of this story centers.

On occasion, the name of an important person in the resistance story will be introduced with the phrase "referred to as." This means the person existed in real life, but the name of the person was not remembered by Eta. In particular, in the cases of non-Jewish Poles who helped her directly, Eta purposely did not want to know their actual names. With Poland under the brutal occupation of Nazi Germany during World War II, being discovered by the Nazis as a person helping Jews was highly dangerous and, if caught, could lead to one's execution.

This also meant that if Eta was ever captured in her own risky and dangerous work as a partisan, she would not know the real names of the local Poles who had been helping out to ever give them up under torture.

Poland Between WWI and WWII

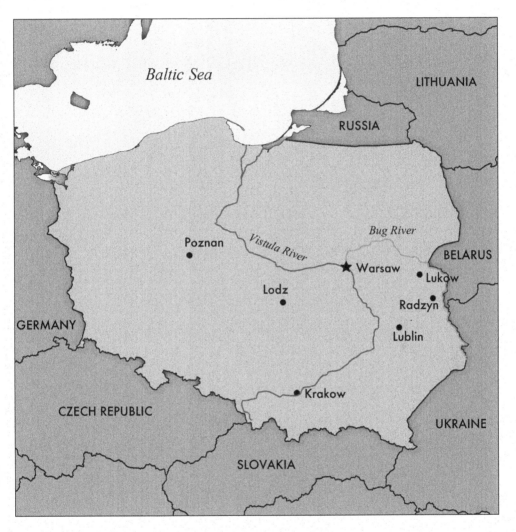

Modern Poland

$\mathcal{I}$ntroduction

Who doesn't like a good story? Stories can entertain us, but they can also inspire and educate us. In fact, stories can give us important messages and teach valuable lessons for our lives today and in the future. I've got such a story for you here.

Imagine This Scenario

To start, imagine the following situation with its three aspects. Think how you would deal with the situation if you were in it. Your country has been invaded and swiftly conquered by a foreign power. This power has a reputation for cruelty. While your home and your family, as well as your relatives living nearby, are fine at the moment, the invasion caused much destruction in towns and cities as well as civilian casualties. Just go out your front door and you can see the death and destruction in your own community. How would you deal with this situation?

In addition, this conquering power has designated a small percentage of your country's population as part of the Other and segregates these Other people into their own enclaves. Movement in and out of these enclaves is restricted, and food supplies have become limited in them. These enclaves have been set up in different cities around your country, including in your own town. By the way, you, your family, and extended family members have been designated as part of this Other group and are now crowded into one of these enclaves. How would you deal with this situation?

Furthermore, much of the rest of the population of your conquered nation is indifferent to the plight of those in the Other group, and some are downright hostile to them. In fact, some of your fellow citizens have gladly joined in to assist the administration of this foreign power to regulate and control the activities of the Other people. The message from this new administration is that anyone who tries to help these Other people will be arrested and imprisoned, and these Other people will be fine as long as they cooperate and join in work details. Yet you have seen in your own town some from the Other group who went off into a work detail and never returned. The word out there is that these people were executed. How would you deal with this situation?

If you are struggling to come up with good answers on how you would deal with this scenario, you are not alone. Even if you thought about escaping your enclave into the dangerous and hostile unknown, where would you go? Who could you count on to help you? What would you do with your family members, especially children and elderly parents?

This imaginary scenario was once real, and it happened in a period known as the Holocaust. The Holocaust began in 1933 in Germany with the rise of Adolf Hitler and his Nazi Party gaining power. Before World War II broke out in Europe during September 1939, Austria and Czechoslovakia had been taken over by Nazi Germany. By the time the United States entered World War II in December 1941, Nazi Germany had conquered and controlled most of Europe. The mass murder phase of the Holocaust was now in full operation. That small percentage of the European population now trapped under the grip of Nazi Germany, those of the Other group, who were the number one target on Hitler's list of inferiors and undesirables, the Jews.

They faced the impossible odds described here. Eta Chait was a young Jewish woman in her 20s at the time. Despite these most difficult circumstances, she not only escaped her enclave—the ghetto—but was also involved in an all-Jewish armed resistance unit and was even part of its leadership.

The Uniqueness of This Story

Eta Chait's story is not only unique because it is about resistance in the face of a nearly impossible and extremely adverse situation, but also because many of the stories of resistance in the Holocaust have not received much attention over the years. In particular, the subject of the Holocaust covered through books, education, and even films falls into three categories:

- *The history of the tragedy and the evil psychology of its perpetrators.*

Many big thick books have been written in this first category, which is often the main emphasis in school textbooks and what gets taught in history classes. For learning about what happened in this tragic period, all are very important.

- *The individual stories of survivors or those who did not survive.*

As Holocaust survivors have aged and started to pass away, many now have been willing to share their tragic stories. The two most widely read books in this second category are *Night*, Nobel Peace Prize winner Elie Wiesel's horrific story of surviving the concentration camps, and *The Diary of Anne Frank*, the journal of a young Jewish girl's attempt to survive in hiding. In fact, these books have been the two most widely read books of all Holocaust genre and are often found in the curriculum of many English classes at the middle school and high school levels. These individual stories of survival and loss are also very critical to a thorough understanding of the struggles of those entrapped by the Holocaust.

- *The stories of resistance and rescue.*

This third category on the subject of the Holocaust is least recognized, least known, and least taught. It contains the stories of the Jews and non-Jews who stood up against the Nazi tyranny to try and save the lives of Jews from certain death. These are the stories of ordinary people, not governments, or armies. They are the people who fought back despite the tremendous odds against them, or who worked to help Jews escape to safe destinations, or who helped Jews hide from the Nazi authorities and their collaborators.

This book represents my second book in this category of resistance and rescue. My other book in this category eventually led me to write this story about Eta Chait. *The Righteous Few: Two Who Made a Difference* is the true story of a young married Dutch Christian couple named Frans and Mien Wijnakker. During World War II when the Netherlands was under the brutal occupation of Nazi Germany, this couple got involved when most people did not, and saved the lives of more than two dozen Jews from certain death. It is a story in which I also have a meaningful personal connection, as you will discover when you read the book.

The Righteous Few: Two Who Made a Difference has put me on an unexpected journey, now ten years and counting. I have had hundreds of events including speaking engagements and book discussions on this story across multiple cities in the United States and one in Canada, too. As the journey has evolved, I have given other related presentations under the umbrella of Heroes in the Holocaust, focusing on Jews who offered forceful resistance and other non-Jews and Jews who worked to rescue Jews from the clutches of Nazi tyranny. For the last few years, Eta Chait's life has been one of the people of resistance and rescue I have included in these talks.

These engagements have been in a wide variety of venues: places of faith, places of work, places of learning, places of service, and many others. Whether I have spoken directly on my first book in this area or about other Holocaust heroes and heroines, I commonly receive these comments:

- Amidst the horrific tragedy of the Holocaust, I didn't know there was anything positive.

- Thank you for these inspirational stories of courage and compassion.

- How come we haven't been hearing stories about these courageous people; they are very important for people to know about.

- Keep sharing these stories. They teach valuable lessons and remind us of the good in people.

- In today's often polarizing political climate, these stories of people standing up for themselves and for others and doing the right thing are needed now more than ever.

These comments apply to Eta Chait and her resistance story. She became part of the leadership of an all-Jewish partisan unit in the forests of Poland during World War II and the Holocaust. Partisan was the term used for those Jews and non-Jews who went underground, taking up arms to engage in combat and defense activities against the Germans and their collaborators throughout all of Nazi-controlled Europe. By the time the United States got directly involved to fight in World War II, at the start of 1942 when the war in Europe was already over two years into it, Nazi Germany and its allies in the Axis Powers controlled most of Europe. Beyond a few countries allowed to remain neutral at this time (Sweden, Switzerland, Spain, Portugal, Turkey), only Great Britain and the Soviet Union were still standing trying to fight Germany and its allies. Both were losing badly at the time, before the United States even began to get its military involved in the fight. As a consequence, the odds were stacked against anyone who got into any kind of partisan unit in German-occupied areas, even more so, Jews who were the top target of the Nazi extermination list.

The Importance This Story Provides

This book has an added importance. It is meant to counter the appalling bias that has gone on for many years that "the Jews went like lambs to the slaughter." This blame-the-victim bias is not typically applied to other people who became victims in this genocide or any other ones that have occurred before or since the Holocaust—Armenia, Cambodia, Rwanda.

For example, during the Holocaust in the fall of 1939 in Poland, the Germans initiated what Nazi officials referred to as Intelligenzaktion. After Poland had succumbed to the invasion of Nazi Germany by the end of September 1939, over the next three months some 60,000 people who the German conquerors viewed as part of Poland's political and social elite, predominantly Catholic Poles, were rounded up and murdered. This intelligentsia or elite consisted of former government officials, former military officers, professors, teachers, priests, doctors, and wealthy landowners. This action was before Germany carried out its murderous plan of the Jews. So did these members of the Polish intelligentsia go like "lambs to the slaughter?"

No victim of the Holocaust—Roma, Sinti, gay, disabled, communist, political dissident, person of Slavic heritage, Red

Army prisoner of war from the Soviet forces, and Jew—asked, "What line do I go on so I can be killed?" Such bias of blaming the victim tends to absolve the murderers and their helpers of their responsibility for committing these heinous acts on innocent people.

Before terrorism became the widely-used term applied today to rogue groups around the world, there was Nazi Germany. It was a terrorist state that by 1942 had its murderous grip on nearly all of Europe. And the Germans had help. In nearly every country they conquered throughout Europe during the war, the Germans had much help from the local populations in the roundup, deportation, and execution of Jews. These were the collaborators—members of local law enforcement, members of government, and regular citizens who marched along and actively participated in the persecution and genocide. Furthermore, the Germans commonly used imports, especially Ukrainians, Lithuanians, and Romanians, in helping run the concentration camps and serving in the murder squads, known as the Einsatzgruppen, throughout Eastern Europe.

In addition to the German perpetrators and their collaborators in these crimes were vast millions more in these conquered countries who looked the other way and even reported Jews on the run to the authorities. Bystander is the term commonly used for these people in Holocaust education efforts today. Do we hear blame about them for allowing the lambs to be slaughtered?

This blame-the-victim bias perpetuates the great myth that there was little to no Jewish resistance during the Holocaust. This is a wrong assumption and all the more reason for Eta's story to be shared so as to repudiate this myth of ignorance. All the more reason that this book will provide you with a broader picture of what was happening to Jews during this period of Nazi terrorism that makes any resistance and rescue effort an amazing feat—one that should be publicized, applauded, and never forgotten.

So I introduce you to Eta Chait. To most of her friends and family members, she is better known as Eta Wrobel, her married name. Chait is her maiden name. She was, after all, married to Henry Wrobel for more than 60 years and lived most of her adult years with Henry in the New York City area, where they raised three children. She passed away in 2008 at the age of 92.

But the crux of this story is about her time before she emigrated to New York in the late 1940s. It's about her time growing up in a place called Lukow, Poland and, in particular, her time in that country when it was conquered by Nazi Germany. This was a time, when despite great risk and danger, she actively made efforts to resist this tyranny and help others, especially Jews. In May 1943, Eta escaped the Lukow ghetto as it was going through its final liquidation and made her way into the forests. She became, by age 27, one of the leaders of an all-Jewish partisan unit there. Through this time period of the war and through all the harrowing and amazing experiences she went through working to battle and save others, experiences she never asked for, this remarkable young woman was known as Eta Chait.

So Despite insurmountable odds and tragedy all around, there were thousands of Jews who resisted the terrorism of Nazi Germany and all its collaborators. Eta Chait was one of them. Enjoy the journey getting to know this woman of valor.

The Beginnings in Lukow

Summer of 1964, London, England: One of Europe's largest cities and a popular place that attracts tourists from around the world. Those double decker hop-on, hop-off buses are a good way for tourists to get a view of some of the famous sites in London.

One Gutsy Woman

On a nice sunny day that summer, two American tourists from New York City board one of these tour buses in London—a woman in her late 40s, and her 14-year-old daughter. As they board the bus to buy tickets, they are greeted with a smile and a few friendly words from the bus driver who will guide them through the streets of London. The daughter, named Anna, is excited to be on the bus and runs to get a seat with her mother trailing behind. The mother is no more than five feet, three inches in height. If you heard her speak, you would detect an accent, indicating that she probably came from somewhere else before now living in the United States.

The bus is fairly filled with chatty tourists. A few minutes into the ride with Anna smiling as she looks out the window to see the city sites, two male youths get on the bus. They are likely in their late teens. Anna would recall, years later, that these two youths had a skinhead-type appearance—crew cuts, white T-shirts, worn jeans, and a tattoo or two visibly showing on their arms and necks. Scowls are seen on their faces. As the driver approaches to collect their tickets, one of the males pokes at his shoulder and the two youths raise their voices and start to verbally taunt the driver with comments such as, "This driver is a black man. We have a black man on this bus." Even when they pay their tickets and take a seat, the two teens shout again, "Black man, hey black man!"

The passengers on the bus go completely silent. Everyone is either staring out the window or looking down. Great tension fills the whole bus. But this somewhat diminutive woman from New York, Anna's mother, is not looking the other way. She starts breathing heavily, almost heaving, with her eyes looking like laser beams. Then in a very loud voice while pointing directly at the two males, she exclaims, "Yes, you're right. We see that he's black. And yes, we see that he's a man. But what are you? Neither of you are a man. This too we can see. So how about you leave us all be now!"

The two skinhead-looking youths are stunned and fall silent. They immediately sink down in their seats. A couple of minutes later, as the bus comes to its next stop, the two male youths quickly depart. The tension on the bus disappears as the passengers resume their chatter, enjoying their ride in London. A little while later, the mother and daughter from New York are ready to get off the bus. As they pass by the bus driver, he greets them with a warm smile, and in his Caribbean accent says a big thank you and wishes them well.

So who was this gutsy woman with some kind of European-sounding accent who put these two youths in their place? Her name, Eta Wrobel; Eta Chait before she was married. Eta had dealt with a lot tougher and more threatening situations in her life prior to this bus trip encounter with what to her were just two punks. The roots of her courage and toughness, along with that accent, came from a place called Lukow, Poland.

The Town of Lukow

Prior to the start of World War II, Lukow was a town with a population of little more than twelve-and-a-half thousand people. Nearly half of its residents at the time were Jews like Eta and her family. Lukow is located in southeastern Poland about 75 miles due east and slightly south from the country's capital and largest city, Warsaw. Not far from this small city to its east is the major body of water in the area, the Bug River. It is the fourth longest river in the country of Poland. Today it forms part of the border between the countries of Poland and Ukraine. In the 1920s and 1930s, as Eta was growing up, people did not travel too much from their own towns or villages. But for the people of Lukow, if they ventured out to visit or shop in the nearest sizable city, it would have been Lublin. Lublin is the main city of Lublin Province, of which Lukow is a part, and is located a little less than 60 miles due south and slightly west of Lukow. Just prior to the start of the war, the city of Lublin had just over 120,000 inhabitants.

In its own locale, Lukow was the main center of activity and commerce. Surrounding it were deep forests and more than 20 little villages with many individual farms—countryside at its best. If someone did not know his or her way around, getting lost in the woods would not be hard to do. So for people who resided in these villages and the outlying countryside area, Lukow was their big city.

Eta's Family Roots

In Lukow, during 1913, a Jewish couple got married. The husband was named Pinchas Ben Chaim Chait and his wife was Shaindel Goldberg. She was 18 years old at the time of their wedding; Pinchas was nearly 10 years older. They had both been born and raised in Lukow. They had met a year before. She had caught his eye as a beautiful young lady he had wanted to get to know right away. He soon boldly asked her out on a date rather than work through a matchmaker, as was sometimes the custom in Jewish circles. She, of course, accepted as she found the lean and tall Pinchas quite attractive and admired his intelligence and kind-hearted nature too. You might say it was love at first sight. So when they got married within a year, it came as no surprise.

Shaindel had an older sister named Gitel who was married before her to a Jewish man named Benjamin Gontarsky. Shortly after their marriage, Benjamin went off to London and was able to get work and residency there, sending for his new wife to join him in 1912. England provided a far better life for Jews in this time period than Poland, which was part of Russia. Had Shaindel and her new husband Pinchas known what lay ahead in the 1930s, especially by September 1939, maybe they too would have worked to move to England. Gitel, her husband, and their family of two children would survive World War II.

Nonetheless, Pinchas and Shaindel set out to raise a large family. Over the next 20 years of their marriage, they would have ten children—an even mix of five boys and five girls. The household seemed like there was always a new baby around or on the way. But with a house full of children, the older ones played a role in helping care for the younger ones. Pinchas and Shaindel were loving parents and instilled a closeness for one another among all the siblings. They in turn would refer to their parents by affectionate Yiddish names for father and mother, Tateh and Mammushe respectively.

In 1914, the first child was born, a son named Chaim Schulem. Everyone referred to him as Schulem. In less than a year-and-a-half, on April 2, 1916, child number two was born. This was their oldest daughter named Hela Eta. Early on, she went by her middle name, Eta, and forever after throughout her life. The rest of the siblings would follow in close order.

Adding to the loving and close-knit family Eta grew up with was a third-generation person who lived in the Chait home, Grandmother Fraida, Eta's maternal grandmother. Being ill and widowed, Eta's parents took her into their home not long after they got married. She stayed with the family until her death at the age of 84; she was a fond part of Eta's early youth.

Eta's Early Years

Unlike the next two siblings in birth order—sisters Miriam Sara, usually called Mara, born two years after Eta, and Fraida, born approximately four years after that—Eta showed little interest in learning how to cook or doing other household chores that girls were expected to master as they grew into young women. This straying from the traditional role of housewife and homemaker caused worry for Mammushe, Eta's mother.

From an early age Eta often played with boys. She had a tomboy spirit, as she would refer to it. She was very athletic and good in any physical activity or sport she got involved in, from riding bikes to playing volleyball and especially football, or soccer as Americans call it. This meant she had to play with boys. Such activities were not ones that girls of the 1920s and 1930s participated in, especially Jewish girls. She was often one of the best players in these pick-up soccer matches, so the boys did not mind at all having her on their team. She also was not afraid to get herself dirty, playing in the streets, ball fields, gardens, and orchards in and around Lukow, even in the mud after a rainy day—much to the consternation of her parents.

In addition, Eta was a top student at school. She attended the local public school in Lukow with the Polish Catholic children, not something Jewish children did too commonly in Poland. She was an avid reader and had a knack for getting high marks in all her subjects. She learned and spoke Polish as well as Yiddish, which was the first language for most Polish Jews. Her academic prowess and intelligence led her to skip some early grades in school and graduate from secondary school (high school) when she was just 15 years old.

So here was this young girl growing up as one of the best athletes and smartest kids in her class, with a bold spirit on top of it. Eta was not the quiet and shy type. She had a certain presence that attracted both boys and girls to her from an early age. If there was a play activity or school activity to be organized and led, Eta was often the one the other children counted on to make this happen. As she recalled in her memoir, when she was old enough to dance with boys, she would be the one to lead.

This bold leadership spirit Eta showed was nurtured most by her father, Tateh. He saw something special and different in her and encouraged her to do well in school and get the best education she possibly could. He praised her for her top grades and for any activity where she showed leadership. Her tomboy tendencies did not bother him at all. One might say Pinchas Chait had an enlightened outlook far beyond the time period in which he was raising his family.

He knew Eta had certain aspirations to make something of herself beyond the traditional role of housewife and homemaker, and he wanted to see this happen for his oldest daughter. Now outwardly, to show support for his wife, Mammushe, he would join in the laments on how Eta was not acting lady-like. But none of that deterred Eta one bit from being her own person, which contributed to a strong woman in the making.

Growing up, Eta's best friend was her older brother Schulem. Despite being close in age, sibling rivalry was not part of their relationship at all; in fact, quite the opposite. They did many activities together, and sometimes her friends mixed with his friends as they would do activities as a group. At parties, Schulem was the one who took the lead, making sure all the boys danced with all the girls so no one was left out. As teens, they sometimes went on double dates together. They were the ones who made sure their younger brothers and sisters made it to school on time or got to where they needed to be. In their social outings, they often brought along one of their young siblings as part of the activity with their friends. The close-knit nature of their family made them think nothing about having a little child to join in with their friends. It was their way of helping their parents in caring for the younger siblings.

Eta adored Schulem. As he grew from a teen to a young man, he was in her eyes tall, handsome, very good-natured, and very popular in school. He was also tough. Schulem was unafraid to stand up for himself and act against any slight of anti-Semitism. He did not seek fights but did not back down from them either. Fellow youth in school learned not to mess around with Schulem Chait and therefore by extension, with his sister Eta. When the 1930s rolled around and gangs of non-Jewish youth sought to bully Jews they saw walking in the streets in Lukow, they quickly went the other way when they saw Schulem and his friends coming by. Eta liked this sense of protection her big brother provided.

Since Eta excelled in all her studies, including her Jewish studies, she was the one who helped Schulem learn his Torah portion in Hebrew for his Bar Mitzvah, that rite of passage to adulthood in Judaism when a boy turns 13. Schulem expressed great appreciation for her help, which greatly pleased Eta.

Eta's family was considered middle class. Her father ran a sizable bakery in town that had a good reputation for its quality of goods and service. His customers were both Jews and Catholics of Lukow. Many Jews in Lukow were poor. So Eta's family was more well off than most other Jews in town.

Eta's Early Influences

Eta's father was a community leader and believed in service to others. He was part of the town council of Lukow, a member of the school board, and a leader in the main Jewish community organizations, where caring for the poor with various charitable activities was part of their efforts. Pinchas worked hard and was well respected by Jew and non-Jew alike in Lukow.

When Eta and her siblings became old enough to start primary school, they pitched in and helped out at their father's bakery after school. It was truly a family business. In fact, when Schulem and her sister Mara finished their formal education in their teen years, both then worked full-time helping run the bakery and its business operations and retail stores. This allowed Pinchas to put his time into all the community service activities he did, while keeping his viable and profitable business running well. The close-knit sense of family for the Chaits went beyond the inside of their household.

Eta's experience in working after school in her father's bakery helped her learn customer service. Anyone who came into the store was greeted in a friendly manner and given whatever help they needed to make their purchase run smoothly. As a young teen, around age 15, Eta started seeing a young woman come into the bakery fairly often to buy cookies. The woman, whose name she never knew, would become curious seeing Eta reading a book whenever she came into the store. She would strike up a conversation with Eta about what she was reading. By appearance and gossip around town, Eta knew this woman was a prostitute who was now living with her local pimp in town. When this woman asked how she could obtain the books that Eta was reading, Eta knew she would probably not be treated very well if she went to the local library. Learning early on from both of her parents to treat everyone with kindness, Eta made an arrangement with this young woman; she, Eta, would go to the library and pick up books for her. The woman would then rendezvous at the bakery on the afternoons Eta was on duty, and pick up a book with her cookies—an act of kindness that would not be forgotten by this prostitute.

As mentioned previously, one other important influence in Eta's early life was her Grandmother Fraida, whom Eta loved dearly. Near six years old when her grandmother died, Eta always remembered the day of her passing distinctly. That morning her grandmother asked Eta's mother to light two candles for her, saying when they flickered out so would she. And that's exactly what happened. This spiritual passing would serve as a source of inspiration and strength for Eta, helping her survive and fight through the worst times of her life in the years to come—the Holocaust. As the 1930s rolled around and Eta was growing to be a young woman, the doom and darkness for Jews in Europe had begun—including in her native Poland.

2

Poland and Its Jews Prior to Eta Coming into the World

"It was the best of times; it was the worst of times." This line from the famous book, *Tale of Two Cities* by Charles Dickens aptly describes the history and life of Jews in Poland prior to the birth of Eta Chait in 1916. Knowing what came before her is critical in understanding the danger that lay ahead. Poland's past as a country and as a home for Jews had great bearing on the impending future of the world as Eta was growing up in the 1920s and 1930s, even before World War II. Here is a brief historical perspective to help understand this big-picture.

Jewish Life in Poland: The Early Years

Anti-Semitism in its ugliest forms of discrimination, persecution, castigation, and violence toward Jews existed throughout Europe for hundreds of years, long before Adolf Hitler came out of Austria to become the absolute dictator of Nazi Germany in the 1930s. Jews were a small minority. They were "the others" who did not go along with the wave of Christianity that started to take a firm hold throughout Europe by the fifth century of the common era. Yet there were some "best of times" for Jews in Poland. Yes, contrary to popular belief, there were good periods for Jewish life in Poland. Those led to the Poland in which Eta grew up—one that was the center for Jewish life, both religiously and culturally, in the world. Eta's Poland in the 1930s had more than one-third the population of all of Europe's Jews in it, and Jews were a little less than ten percent of the total population of Poland. Nowhere else in Europe were Jews, as a minority group, anywhere near this size or presence.

The development of this significant Jewish life in Poland traces its roots to when Jews first arrived in Poland from other parts of Europe in medieval times, also called the Middle Ages. Jews came to escape harsh persecution and extreme violence elsewhere and came because they were actually invited.

During the Middle Ages—the period of history running from the late 400s with the final collapse of the Roman Empire until near 1500 when the Renaissance and Age of Enlightenment took over—wherever Jews lived throughout Europe, metaphorically they faced a huge unwelcome mat. As the main non-Christian minority in the continent, there were stringent restrictions segregating where they lived—where the term ghetto comes from—and limiting the occupations in which they could work. On top of that, they were considered Christ killers, as preached by the dominant influence of the time period, the Roman Catholic Church. In addition, it warned its parishioners to watch out for Jews as they may take Christian children for sacrifice to drink their blood and use it in their unleavened bread during Passover—the ridiculous conspiracy theory called blood libel.

An even worse time for Jews was the Crusades. From the late 11th century into the late 13th century, as Christian armies marched across Europe on their way to recapture the Holy Land (Israel today) from Muslim rule, they sometimes warmed up by attacking Jewish communities along the way, bringing much murder and destruction. Jews were easy scapegoats for whatever ills or problems were happening in a given society, small or large. The worst was when the widespread epidemic known as the Black Plague or Black Death hit much of Europe in the 1300s and 1400s. As millions of Europeans died from this disease, thousands of Jews were massacred by mobs. Someone had to be blamed for this terrible plague.

Furthermore, Jews were expelled from England in 1290, from France in 1306 and then again in 1394, from many of the German states in the mid 1300s, and from Hungary in 1376. In 1492 as Christopher Columbus sailed the ocean blue for King Ferdinand and Queen Isabella of Spain, the Spanish Inquisition was in full force. The Catholic monarchs of Spain wanted a purely Catholic country. Under the guise of a judicial inquiry known as the Inquisition, ridding the country of non-Catholics, primarily the Muslim Moors and Jews, became the emphasis. From this, Jews were either expelled from the country, murdered, or forced to convert to Christianity if they wanted to stay. Portugal followed suit before the decade was out.

So where did many Jews in Europe go to escape this hostile climate they faced? Poland. It was the place of safe refuge. The first Jews started to settle in Poland as early as 1096. During the next three centuries, the flow of Jews into Poland continued steadily. In fact, they were invited to come by the rulers and aristocracy of Poland. As the kingdom of Poland attempted to unify its regions, it sought to promote economic growth. Beyond the noble class and royalty, most Poles had little formal education and were basically illiterate. Many of the Jews coming in from other parts of Europe were educated and had skills. They served as managers for the estates of the nobility. They helped with financial management and in lending money—a business practice the Catholic Church viewed as sinful, keeping most

Christians away from engaging in this work. They served as court advisers. Some Jews were doctors, merchants, traders, and artisans.

While many of the Jews coming to settle in Poland were poor like the Polish peasants, this influx of talent was greatly welcomed by those Poles in positions of power and wealth who were pleased to see the growth of commerce coming from it. In fact, during the reign of one Polish king known as Casimir the Great, who ruled from 1333 to 1370, Jewish life in Poland was greatly enhanced. He reinforced a charter created in 1264 and extended it to all provinces under his authority, granting Jews full rights for practicing their religion, for work, for owning property, and for where they chose to reside. His rulings ran contrary to the powerful preachings of the Catholic Church which had no tolerance for non-Christians, especially Jews. Casimir the Great encouraged good relations between Jews and Catholic Poles; a view that suggested equality and engagement were keys for Poland's economic and urban development.

Like other Europeans, strains of prejudice and resentment against Jews did not automatically disappear among Poles despite these rulings and proclamations from the crown. Comments expressing disapproval of Jews from the Catholic clergy were heard along with complaints among peasants who did not like working for a Jewish administrator. Resentment by Polish merchants and craftsmen against this "unfair economic competition" from Jews was sometimes voiced as well. Occasional accusations of blood libel saw a few incidents of attacks and murders of Jews. As cities like Warsaw and Krakow grew in the late 1400s, they enacted restrictions against Jews residing in their municipalities. Yet, despite this existence of anti-Semitism, the protective nature of the royalty and noble class gave Jews coming into Poland during the last few centuries of the Middle Ages a sense of comfort and belonging.

The Formation of Strong Jewish Life in Poland

During the 1500s and 1600s, the migration of Jews into Poland continued. As this migration was occurring, a trend that began before 1500 continued to grow during this period. Jews created their own villages, sections within towns, and townships—in Yiddish referred to as shtetls—throughout Poland. These shtetls became autonomous entities for Jews to not only survive in greater peace but to also thrive both religiously and culturally. These townsfolk built institutions for religious practice and study. The Yiddish language and development of it in literature, music, and drama became a part of the cultural fabric for Jewish life in Poland. Jews set up their own councils called kehillah that administered governmental and legal affairs inside the shtetls. Jews were still answerable to the crown and paid taxes to it like all Polish citizens. But this segregated life by choice, which gave Jewish people the opportunity to truly live freely as Jews, was permitted by the authorities of Poland.

Interesting enough, even by the 1920s and 1930s as Eta was growing up, Yiddish was the main language spoken in her house, as was true for the vast majority of Jews throughout Poland then. The fact that Eta could speak Polish fluently was somewhat unusual in her early1900s world.

By the 1700s, it is estimated that over eighty percent of Jews in Poland, from rich to poor, lived in these self-contained communities. Jews involved in commerce and trade certainly interacted with the non-Jewish Poles for doing business, but their shtetls were their world for living and raising their families so as to forge a strong Jewish identity. Jews were the largest minority in Poland during the 1700s, estimated to be ten percent of the total population, and the largest Jewish population to be found in any country in the world at this time. More importantly, the Jewish communities of Poland with their educational

institutions for Jewish religious scholarship and their synagogues for Orthodox practice of their faith were viewed as the
role model for Jews around the world. Even Jews from other
parts of the world came to study in Poland at the religious acad-
emies for youth, in the late teens and older, called yeshivas. This
was the "best of times."

Life Grows Harder For Jews in Poland

But major cracks in this rich Jewish life began to appear in the
mid-1600s. Uprisings by the Cossacks, mostly Ukranians not
happy to be a minority now incorporated into Poland, led to
great violence in Poland for a couple of years. Jews were among
their targets, with an estimate of nearly 100,000 dying in these
attacks. Subsequently, conflicts and invasions by armies from
Sweden and Russia led to further weakening of the Polish econ-
omy and its government. This downward spiral for the country
of Poland continued throughout the 1700s, with Jews adversely
affected as a consequence.

By 1795, Poland's existence as its own independent country
was no more. It had been carved up by three neighboring powers: a small section was ceded to Austria, another small section
went to the German state of Prussia (the various German states
would unify as the nation of Germany in 1871), and the vast
majority of people and area fell under the control of Russia.

The royal rulers of the Russian empire, known as the tsars,
came down hard on the Jews they inherited. Starting with the
rule of Catherine the Great, what was called the Pale of Settle-
ment was created. This restricted where Jews could live, greatly
limited the occupations in which they could work, and curtailed
where Jewish merchants could do business. In brief, this meant,
in most cases, that Jews from what was Poland had to stay in
their designated towns or shtetls and were not permitted to come

to the main part of Russia at all for any purpose. As a result, poverty became a way of life now for many more Jews than before. In addition, resentment and hostility from their fellow Poles, very angered by the takeover of these outside powers, simmered at a high level toward Jews. Jews, to many of them, were just foreigners with questionable loyalties who did not belong in the Polish nation they desired to regain one day.

Interesting enough, the last Polish insurrection against this Russian takeover was led in 1794 by Tadeusz Kosciuszko, a Polish hero in the American Revolutionary War, whose army included Jewish fighters. It did not succeed. Yet, despite this restrictive and hostile climate, with mass violent attacks known as pogroms occurring occasionally from the 1880s and beyond, Jews in their shtetls were still able to maintain their religious and cultural life. The Yiddish language was still thriving among the vast majority of Jews.

As the Twentieth Century Comes To Poland

As the twentieth century rolled around, changes were happening in Poland and along with these changes, alternative paths for Jews emerged in carrying out their lives. These changes would have much influence on Eta in her youth and upbringing. A growing restlessness to have their own nation again was intensifying among Poles, especially those under the rule of Russia. With this rising nationalism came political movements, such as socialism and communism in Russia and elsewhere around Eastern Europe, including Poland, with some Jews getting involved. The Bund, a Jewish socialist movement, took hold. Another political movement called Zionism drew in some Jews. This new movement's objective was to regain a Jewish country in the area of its ancient homeland in the Middle East, then called Palestine (today Israel) and part of the Ottoman Empire until 1918.

Taking a different path, some Jews in Poland began to assimilate and move away from an Orthodox or devout religious life. Many people among Polish intellectuals and liberals favored seeing Jews take on this secular or non-religious life. As part of this secular way of life, Jews in the cities and others who were able to work their way to these urban areas, sought a university education and began to enter professions such as law and medicine.

This ever-changing yet politically turbulent time was the world into which Eta Chait would be born in 1916. While a large majority of Jews in Poland still lived in their separate towns, maintaining their Orthodox religious lifestyles, and often living in poverty, diversity among Jews was growing.

Then World War I hit Europe in 1914, including Poland. Forces from Germany and Austria occupied the territory of Poland. They were part of the Central Powers along with the Ottoman Empire who fought against the Allied Powers that included Russia, Great Britain, France, and eventually in 1917, the United States. By 1917, Russia had become engulfed in its own internal war, the Bolshevik Revolution, which led to the rise of the first communist-run country called the Soviet Union. On November 11, 1918, World War I ended with the Central Powers defeated.

As a result, opportunity came knocking at Poland's door. With foreign troops off their soil, the Poles, led by a man named Jozef Pilsudski, declared independence. The rebirth of the nation of Poland had begun. At the same time, in the town of Lukow, Eta Chait was in her infancy. Were the "best of times" to return to Eta's homeland, for her fellow Jews in it, and for her as she would begin to grow up?

3

$\mathcal{T}$he Interwar Years in Poland

O n November 10, 1918, Jozef Pilsudski, who had been a leader in the Polish Socialist Party before the war, returned to Warsaw. He had been recently released from a prison in Germany. The very next day, the Great War was officially declared over. (Since no one knew then about World War II coming in slightly more than 20 years, "the war to end all wars" was known as the Great War rather than World War I as we refer to it today.) With a power vacuum now existing in Poland—German and Austrian forces had evacuated by this time, and Russian forces the year before—on November 11th, Pilsudski declared the rebirth of an independent nation of Poland with himself as head of the new government.

Political Turmoil and Its Impact on the Jews of Poland

In the 1890s as Polish nationalism and the eagerness to push out the foreign occupying powers of their land grew—the empires of Austria-Hungary, Germany, and especially Russia—two Polish political movements emerged to lead this charge. One was the National Democratic Party, commonly called Edecja, led by Roman Dmowski. He and his party were considered right wing, and they were vocally anti-Semitic and marginalized other minority groups too within Poland. The other party was the Polish Socialist Party, called Sanacja, led by Jozef Pilsudski. Prior to the start of the Great War, Pilsudski's political activities in Poland under Russian rule had landed him in prison a couple of times. But Pilsudski and his Socialists had gotten a head start on Dmowski and his Endecja Nationalists. Even though he had no formal military background, Pilsudski had organized a Polish army when the Great War broke out in 1914; Jewish soldiers were part of it. He formed an alliance to support the Austrian and German forces that came in to Poland to fight the Russian army in hope that these countries would support Polish independence in return. Germany, tired of his independence demands, had imprisoned Pilsudski for a little while in the latter stages of the war.

Finally, on November 11, 1918, the Great War was over and Pilsudski, almost age 51, charged ahead to lead a reborn Poland to independence. But the new country was not stable. Despite the euphoria from gaining independence across Poland, the Endecja party's right-wing nationalist fervor spurred pogroms across the country against ethnic minorities, especially Jews. An estimated 100 such rampages and murdering attacks against Jews occurred over the next two-plus months. In 1920, more such pogroms occurred as forces from the new Soviet Union invaded Poland in attempt to retake it, again destabilizing the country. After all, as heard throughout Poland, Jews were really on the side of the Communists. Under Marshal Pilsudski, now carrying the title of commander-in-chief of the Polish armed forces, within a year the Polish army was able to push back the Red Army invaders and retain their new nation. Still, one such pogrom hit Lukow in 1920, causing the murder of 13 Jews there. Young Eta and her family were not harmed.

By the end of June 1919, a peace conference held in Paris to officially end the Great War had concluded with the Allied

Powers enacting the Treaty of Versailles. A wounded Austrian corporal who had served in the German army—some guy named Adolf Hitler—was recuperating in a hospital when the war ended in 1918. He was furious at the punishing terms the treaty enacted on Germany—loss of all colonies overseas, restrictions on its military, reductions of its own national territory, and costly war reparations. At the same time, the Treaty of Versailles redrew the map of Europe and created new countries, such as Czechoslovakia, Yugoslavia, and Poland. Pilsudski won out over Dmowski at the Paris conference as the legitimate representative for the newly-created Poland. He was willing to accept the conditions imposed by the Allied Powers to treat all minorities, including Jews, with freedom and equality. This was not something Dmowski and Endecja could stomach.

Poland Under Pilsudski's Leadership

Pilsudski favored a Poland that allowed equal rights for all its citizens, including the freedom to retain their religion, language, and cultural practices. By 1922, Pilsudski had stabilized Poland and helped it form a democratic government with a constitution granting these rights for all citizens. Jews, like Eta's father, were very glad to see Pilsudski in charge. The new Poland he led was nearly one-third minorities, those not Polish Catholic by origin. In area, it was bigger than the country of Poland today in the 21st century. In addition to the territory that comprises Poland today, the post-World War I nation included parts of areas that are in the countries of Lithuania, Belarus, and Ukraine today. Some ethnic Germans were part of this new Poland. Ukranians were the largest minority group, at approximately 14 percent of the total population.

Jews were the second largest minority in Poland, a little less than 10 percent of the country's population. The other ethnic minorities were found in certain sections of the country, while Jews were interspersed throughout in its cities, towns, and countryside.

By 1923, Pilsudski had stepped away into retirement, allowing colleagues from his party to take over as leaders. When the government seemed to be spiraling back into chaos with labor strikes and rising unemployment occurring, he returned to the forefront and his bloodless coup brought him back into power in 1926. Pilsudski would actually serve in the role of Minister of Defense, allowing his Socialist allies to serve as leaders of the government. But he would remain the power behind the top leadership, holding the country together. Endejca had not gone away and was pushing an agenda to enact anti-Jewish laws, only to be thwarted by Pilsudski and his Sanacja party in Parliament. Jews in Poland voted heavily for Pilsudski's Socialist party. He represented the buffer for them against the return of a harsh, anti-Semitic life in Poland.

Meanwhile, Life in Lukow

Back in Lukow, as Eta came of age to begin school in the early 1920s, she benefitted from the law passed by the newly-created government of Poland that all children must attend school. This meant that Jews, if they chose, could attend government-supported schools. It also meant that Jewish girls now were allowed to receive formal education. In Poland's Jewish history of self-contained communities delivering their own education, boys, not girls, were the students, and they were mostly educated on religious studies. Girls often received informal tutoring; the main job for them was to learn how to be a housewife and homemaker. While only a small percentage of Jews in Lukow attended the public schools after the Great War, Eta was one of them. As she was growing up, she got to know many of the non-Jewish Poles with whom she went to school. Her athleticism and smarts plus an engaging personality and a sense of kindness and respect toward others taught to her by her parents helped Eta get along well with most everyone in and outside of school.

In Lukow, a good many of the Jews lived in one main section of town—typical of most shtetls throughout Poland. This included the Chait family. But, there were no precise borders, and some Jews lived in other parts of town that were mixed with non-Jews. The central market of town was where Jews and non-Jews alike often came together to shop. Many Jewish families in Lukow were poor. However, those involved in crafts and small businesses, like Eta's father with his bakery, commonly had interactions with the non-Jewish Poles in town as part of doing business. Once the new Poland stabilized in the early 1920s, relations between Jews and non-Jews, the Catholic Poles, in town were friendly—often better than was evidenced in many other towns and cities throughout the country.

The Rising Tide of Depression and Fascism

As the decade of the 1930s moved forward, two major forces came sweeping across Europe that would not only adversely impact Jews in Poland, but also specifically Eta and her family in the town of Lukow: the Great Depression and the rise of nationalistic, right-wing sentiments, referred to as fascism. In the early 1930s, at the age of 15, Eta graduated from gymnasium—equivalent to high school. Because she had skipped a couple of grades in her primary school years, she was typically two to three years younger than most of her classmates. Graduation meant it was time to go to work.

But the winds of the Great Depression were now seeping into Poland. Eta's Uncle Moshe, her father's brother, lived in Lodz, the second largest city in the country located about 160 miles due west of Lukow. Moishe worked in the grocery wholesale business. Since tough economic times rendered job prospects bleak in Lukow, at Tateh's urging, Eta moved to Lodz where she had family to stay with, and, through her uncle's connections, got a job in the grocery wholesale business. From managing the books and paying the bills to ordering supplies, Eta worked hard and developed good organizational and business skills. She enjoyed the people she worked with, the cousins she lived with, and the social life of movies, theater, and dances the new city offered. Because she liked to write, she started taking a journalism class at night school. A year or so later as Tateh's bakery business was being hit hard by the Depression, and at the urging of his brother Moishe, Eta's father closed his stores and moved the whole family into a five-room apartment in Lodz. He joined his brother in helping run his grocery wholesale business. Eta's oldest brother Schulem set up his own fruit store in one of the nicer neighborhoods in the city. Life in Lodz seemed to be good for the whole Chait family.

But the Great Depression was taking its toll throughout the world, including Poland. Rising unemployment was hitting the country, and someone had to be blamed for these tough times. In May 1935, Jozef Pilsudski died at the age of 67 from liver cancer. The de facto leader behind the Socialist government was gone. This was not good for Jews. The floodgates of Endecja's anti-Semitic nationalistic agenda now opened up allowing its right-wing ideology to take over in Poland.

This fervor was not unique to Poland. The 1930s saw a rising tide of right-wing fascism and nationalism throughout much of Europe. Under Benito Mussolini, Italy got a head start and had established a fascist dictatorship beginning in 1922. A civil war in Spain starting in 1936 would see victory by its right-wing military dictator Francisco Franco established by 1939. Fascist leaders in Hungary and Romania in the 1930s pushed through anti-Jewish laws restricting rights and economic opportunities for Jews in their countries. A rising tide of fascism, called the Nazi Party, was pushing to gain control in Austria—ultimately coming into power before the decade would end. Even more ominously, the standard bearer for virulent fascism, nationalism, and anti-Semitic actions in Europe, Adolf Hitler and his Nazi Party, rose to power in Germany in 1933. Poland, therefore, was not alone in going after its Jews in the 1930s.

After Pilsudski's passing in 1935, with Pilsudski's formerly moderate Sanacja party going along, Endecja-driven laws came out restricting Jews from working in civil service, banning them from working in state-run industries, limiting their numbers in professions such as law and medicine, and prohibiting them from having booths in public markets. Boycotts were sometimes called for by Endecja party leaders to not shop at any Jewish-owned stores. Violent attacks on Jews started to appear more and more on the streets in towns and cities throughout the country.

Articles in the press, pamphlets, and books proliferated with anti-Semitic rants. Writings and sermons from some of the clergy of the Catholic Church in Poland joined in this growing fervor about the Jewish problem. Jews, after all, as these pernicious publications and preachings stated, were harmful to the economic health of Poland not to mention the moral welfare of its people. And don't forget, Jews were agents of communism, too.

For Jews who wanted to attend university in Poland in the latter half of the 1930s, life on campuses became difficult to outright dangerous. Endecja-inspired thugs and students started instituting a separate Jewish section in classes, meaning—this was the only place Jews could congregate and often just stand if they attended class. If those students or the professors in these classes protested against these intrusions, some were shouted down or even beaten. Such thugs sometimes roamed college campuses looking for Jewish students to attack and beat. In the mid 1920s, enrollment of Jewish students in Polish universities was estimated to be more than 20 percent of the total student population. By 1939, the proportion of Jewish students had dropped to eight percent. Those Jews who could afford it went to study at universities in Western Europe.

The worst of times had come once again for Poland's Jews, with many more now struggling in poverty. Eta and her family in Lodz were doing reasonably well but sensed the tension in the air in this major city. In the late 1930s, Eta started seeing German Jews come to Lodz, escaping the harsh persecution inside Nazi Germany. And she could hear the anti-Semitic complaints among Poles about how the Jews were nothing but trouble and were trying to gain control of everything. Customers would come into the store in which she was working and ask for her view on what do with this "rising Jewish problem," not realizing she was Jewish. With her light brown hair, fair complexion, and the secular-style dress of a young urban woman, Eta did not have the long dress, head covering, or dark features seen with many Orthodox Jews. In addition, she spoke Polish fluently without a Yiddish accent, so people thought she was a Christian.

Talk on the street also contained concern about nearby neighbor Nazi Germany. As Germany was building up its military and annexing Austria and then Czechoslovakia in the late 1930s, with Great Britain and France watching, Poles on the streets in Lodz wondered if a German invasion was imminent. Eta and Tateh, her father, would talk periodically about the tougher life that had come for many Jews in Poland. Tateh voiced his displeasure for the violence and discrimination that was being aimed at Jews, but the biggest concern he had was with that crazy guy Hitler running the show in Germany. He expressed that Germany was a bigger threat to the Jews of Poland than the anti-Semitic Nationalists like Endecja. Eta enjoyed these conversations with Tateh about the greater issues of the day and the fact that he would confide and speak openly to her about these matters that were on his mind. Despite these concerns, Tateh would still encourage Eta to stay strong and work hard.

Like many people during the Great Depression, Eta had gone through a job layoff, but in the late 1930s, she was keeping Schulem's fruit store running as he had been drafted to serve in the Polish army. When the store eventually was forced to close, she joined her father and uncle in their business. Despite these tough times during the Depression and the blame-the-Jews atmosphere in Poland, Eta and her family still had hope that life would get better. But the increasing threat to Poland and to Eta's family and other Jews posed by nearby neighbor Nazi Germany was becoming ever more ominous.

Pinchas and Shaindel Chait, Eta's beloved parents, as
newlyweds starting their lives together in 1913.

The growing Chait family in Lukow, Poland in 1929. Seven children now with three more to come. Young Eta, the second oldest, is standing in the back row, second from the left.

Eta's parents in 1930 while life and family were still good. Mammushe and Tateh respectively, as they were affectionately called in Yiddish by their children.

Eta with her best friend, older brother Schulem, in 1938 as young adults in their 20s before the terror of war from Germany would hit Poland and them.

Eta, on the left, with her then 14-year old daughter Anna visiting English cousin Phillip Gontarsky in London, summer 1964.

A ceremony in Lukow on October 5, 2012 in remembrance of the 70th anniversary when the deportations of the Jews from the Lukow Ghetto by the Nazis to the Treblinka death camp began. The memorial there is the site where the Jewish cemetery of Lukow once was. (*Courtesy of Krzysztof Czubaszek*)

Memorial in Lukow today, by where the main synagogue
once stood, to remember the Jews of the town before the
Holocaust claimed them. *(Courtesy of Krzysztof Czubaszek)*

4

$\mathscr{W}$ar Comes to Poland

In 1934, while Jozef Pilsudski was still alive and helping run the government, Poland had forged a non-aggression pact with Germany at the urging of Adolf Hitler. This ten-year agreement meant that neither country would take steps to attack the other. Pilsudski ignored Hitler's idea of going one step further to form a military alliance that would join together if trouble arose to fight against that evil communist state, the Soviet Union.

The Rising Threat From Nazi Germany

This non-aggression agreement would soon be rendered meaningless. As the 1930s moved ahead, so did Hitler's intention to add to his German empire. In March of 1938 Austria was annexed by Nazi Germany without a shot being fired amidst much cheering from many of Austria's citizens. Hitler still had designs on obtaining more territory, which included Poland. He viewed it as the living space he would need for his German people and growing empire. How to make that happen? Danzig was the answer. Danzig was a German port city on the Baltic Sea, Gdansk as the Poles called it and is is its name today. The Treaty of Versailles that ended World War I took this area away from Germany and designated it as a semi-autonomous city-state. The League of Nations, established after World War I and a kind of precursor to the United Nations today, was given official authority over Danzig. Poland was given administrative and economic oversight of the city since it was now within the north central territory of the newly-created nation of Poland. But the vast majority of people residing in the city of Danzig, as the Germans still called it, were German. When Hitler and his Nazi Party rose into power in Germany in 1933, Nazism began to infiltrate Danzig.

In late October 1938, through Foreign Minister Joachim von Ribbentrop, Germany made its first official demand to the Polish government to cede Danzig to Germany. Since the League of Nations had official jurisdiction over this city-state and Poland did not want this disruption to affect its own land, its government refused Nazi Germany's demand. Roughly a month before this, at a conference in Munich, Germany, European powers Great Britain and France agreed to allow Germany to annex the Sudetenland. The Sudetenland was previously a part of western Czechoslovakia and was a region with a good number of ethnic Germans.

As 1938 was drawing to a close, tensions were running high in Europe, and especially in Poland. The inevitable race towards conflict was on. More demands would come from Nazi Germany throughout 1939 for the Polish government to give over Danzig. In the meantime, on March 15th, German forces marched in and annexed the rest of Czechoslovakia with no shots fired. Britain, France, and Poland grew more nervous. Within a month the three nations formed a mutual protection pact, meaning the British and French would guarantee the sanctity of Poland's borders with force if necessary. By summer 1939, Germany nullified its non-aggression pact with Poland that had been signed five years prior. Since Poland was not cooperating by handing over Danzig and a few other small portions of the country, which was all Germany needed according to Hitler, there was no point in maintaining this agreement any further.

On August 23, 1939, the foreign ministers of Germany and the Soviet Union secretly created a non-aggression pact between their two governments with the approval of their bosses, Adolf Hitler and Joseph Stalin. As part of the deal, Germany would allow the Soviets to act when ready to take the eastern portion of Poland and other areas of Eastern Europe within its sphere or borders (including Ukraine, Byelorussia, and the Baltic States of Lithuania, Estonia, and Latvia). With the Soviet Union now in check, Nazi Germany was ready and able to turn its full attention to taking down Poland. After all, Poland had 3.3 million Jews in its borders, more than one-third of the entire Jewish population of Europe and the second largest Jewish community in the world at the time, next to the United States.

That summer of 1939, in Lodz, Eta and her father's conversations about the political events of the day increased in frequency. Tateh knew that if Germany invaded Poland, which he expected would happen fairly soon, the situation would be very bad for Jews. He was well aware of the persecution of Jews in Germany during the 1930s as well as Kristallnacht in November 1938—the Night of Broken Glass, the two-day rampage and riot targeting Jews across Germany and Austria. Tateh now talked to Eta about being prepared to act. He praised the fighting spirit she had within her, and encouraged her to use it to help herself and others when this imminent danger would come their way.

Germany Starts War

On September 1, 1939, German forces invaded Poland. Two days later the other powers of Europe at that time, Great Britain and France, declared war against Germany. Due to the mutual protection alliance formed with Britain and France earlier in the year, the Poles were excited, expecting to have British and French forces to help them fight off the Germans. To the Poles,

Germany was that big bully that needed to be put in its place, and now they would have powerful allies to help them do it.

But that anticipated military help never showed up. Britain and France remained cautious, so Poland was left on its own to fight the invaders. But the Polish military was overmatched and ill equipped. While it had more than a quarter of a million soldiers, most were on horses with rifles. A cavalry with little artillery and a few serviceable fighter planes was no match for the tanks, armored vehicles, and warplanes the German military brought to the fight. German forces came in fast and hard, bombing Warsaw and other cities around the country early on. Back in Lukow, within the first week, its train station and a few other buildings were bombed, resulting in more than 50 civilian deaths.

On September 17, the Red Army forces of the Soviet Union rolled into the eastern half of the country. The Polish military had limited resources at this point to offer strong resistance against another army in the east. They were now trying to defend Warsaw, the last stronghold still standing, against the Germans. At the same time, the top Polish leaders in the national government and military fled the country. Those who did not get stuck in Romania and went instead to France became the country's government-in-exile.

The Happenings in Lodz

Back in Lodz, where Eta and her family were residing, the situation was tense and bleak. Much to the dismay of many of the citizens in the city, the Polish government and military put no emphasis on defending the city. No Polish forces were to be seen in early September when the German army marched into the city. Lodz, the second largest city in the country, was given up without a fight.

Meanwhile, not long after the war began, Schulem had made his way back to the family in Lodz. He had been deployed with his army unit when a dream came to him one night. It was their grandmother, Fraida, warning him to stay out of the battlefields and get away. He woke up and hid in a trench outside of where his unit was camping, only to witness a short time later German warplanes machine gunning the position where his fellow troops were. Hundreds of Polish soldiers were killed. Amidst the chaos and scattering of soldiers, Schulem scurried away. He felt fortunate to be alive and not long after worked his way back to his family.

Regrettably, Lodz was now occupied by German troops. When they initially marched into the city, Eta saw her father cry for the first time. This strong man, the rock of her family was now in tears. Eta understood why. The reality of Tateh's prediction of doom about what would happen if the Germans came into Poland was now upon them. No words had to be spoken now. Eta, while not crying, felt much uneasiness. That same sense of doom hit her too. She worried about her family and the great uncertainty that lay ahead.

By September 17, mostly Warsaw was all that was left in the country. The city was not yet fully under the grip of the German forces, but it was now under a full siege. The Polish government-controlled radio station issued a call for all able-bodied men to come and help defend Warsaw. Just a couple of weeks before, these same radio broadcasts had been telling the people of Poland that the German army was being repelled by the great military forces of Poland.

Regardless, Eta's father, now more than 50 years old, along with Schulem, now age 25, and Eta's next brother in line, Moishe, not quite 16 years of age, decided to join thousands of volunteers throughout Poland to help in the fight. They did not want to sit idly by if there were still a chance to save Poland from the Germans.

However, along the main road to Warsaw, the German air force was waiting and firing away at these men coming to help defend the city. One such strafing wounded Tateh in the leg. He was captured by the Germans and sent to a military hospital. Schulem and Moishe escaped injury and returned to the family in Lodz. Eta and her fighting spirit went into action. This spirit, greatly nurtured by her father over the years, would not let her sit idly by with her father in the hands of the Germans. In a downtown Lodz hotel, the Germans had established a military headquarters. Eta learned German while in school and was fluent in this language. Despite her pleas in German, two guards outside the entrance to the outpost would not let her in to see the commandant in charge. Eta was not deterred. She waited outside around the corner for a little while. When she saw the guards looking distracted, she dashed into the building and worked her way down to the commandant's office on the first floor. His door was open and without hesitation, in she went.

The German commandant looked quite surprised and not too pleased to see a civilian walking right up to him without any security escort. In her fluent German, Eta quickly told him she was not here to do harm but needed his help. She took off the scarf covering the yellow star on her clothing that Jews in Lodz had been ordered to wear. She then boldly proceeded to tell the officer what had happened to her father and that she needed him to issue an order so he could be released to her. In a confident manner, she stated, "My father is not a soldier. He is merely a good citizen trying to help his country. The fight is now over. He needs now to come home and be with his family. You can do the right thing and make that happen." He smiled at her bold approach and told her he was only helping because of the courage she showed. A few days later Tateh was released and back at home, much to the joy of his family.

The Fall of Poland

By September 28, 1939, Poland had officially surrendered. Its eastern portion was under the control of the Soviet Union, and its western portion was under the control of Nazi Germany. Hans Frank, Hitler's former personal attorney, was put in charge of the German territory as its ruling governor. Poland was once again, and even worse than 140 years before, a conquered and occupied land. The Nazi terror was looming. Panic was in the air for Jews and many Polish Catholics as well. Appropriating the symbol of Judaism, the Star of David, and turning it into a badge of humiliation, the Nazi authorities ordered Jews in Lodz and most other cities to wear the yellow star on their outer clothing or as armbands. In Lodz, Jewish-owned businesses were confiscated. Food was becoming hard to come by for Jews in particular. Talk on the street was that the Nazis would soon confine all the Jews in the city into a ghetto.

Eta's parents decided the best thing to do for the family was to return to Lukow where there were people they knew and trusted. In November 1939, despite the trains being overly crowded and not running on a set schedule and sometimes pushing Jews off when too cramped, the entire Chait family over the course of multiple trips reunited and all made it back to Lukow safely. They were able to settle into the basement area of the building they lived in previously.

Before leaving Lodz, Eta went to say goodbye to a good friend she had made during her time in the city. The friend's name was Lola. She was a Polish Catholic, and she had invited Eta on numerous occasions to share in family dinners at her house. Lola was teary-eyed in saying goodbye to a dear friend who had been her confidant. Lola's mother hugged Eta and then gave her a crucifix that could be worn around her neck. She knew Eta was Jewish but told her that this Catholic symbol might come in handy for her one day—a very insightful prediction.

5

$\mathscr{B}$eginnings of Resistance and Its Challenges

B y the end of September 1939, panic, chaos, and fear marked the lives of people in Poland, and especially Jews, in the western zone under the occupation and control of Nazi Germany. Warsaw, the capital and Poland's largest city with 1.3 million people, was left devastated. The German siege and its heavy bombing killed nearly 40,000 civilians and left an estimated one quarter of its building structures damaged or destroyed.

Early Persecution by the Nazis in Poland

During the last few months of 1939, Jews in Nazi-occupied Poland were ordered to wear an arm band on their clothing with the Star of David on it to identify themselves as Jews when going out in public. Periodic acts of terror and humiliation such as taking scissors to Orthodox Jewish men to cut off their beards, beatings of individual Jews, and indiscriminate shootings and killings of Jews were carried out by the SS (the Schutzstaffel, the brutal security arm of the Nazi machine) in Warsaw and other cities. In addition, some Jewish men were being sent off into forced labor details. Jewish schools and community organizations were being shut down by the Nazi authorities and some Jewish-owned property and businesses were confiscated.

Intelligenzaktion was also carried out over the next six months against many of the elite and educated of Polish society. Some 60,000 non-Jewish Poles were rounded up and executed by the SS. No potential for political opposition would be allowed to exist. Thousands of Poles, Jewish and non-Jewish alike, started fleeing east into the Soviet zone by the latter half of September 1939 while the invasion was still going on, and this migration continued for a few months afterwards. These refugees traveled by car, truck, bicycle, and even by foot with whatever possessions they could take along. The Soviet-controlled territory offered hope as a safer place to be than the German-occupied zone, especially for Jews.

One of those participating in this mass migration was a young Jewish man around the age of 21 by the name of Heniek Wrobel. He had grown up on the outskirts of Lukow and was a distant cousin to Eta and her family. She knew of him because Heniek's older brother, Avram, was a friend of her older brother Schulem. Heniek, later in the war, would serve in the Red Army, the military forces of the Soviet Union.

The key to having this chance at safety was fleeing east and crossing the Bug River, the dividing line between the German and Soviet zones in Poland. However, some of the Jews who got across this dividing line did not stay long. The anguish of being separated from their families was too much, so they returned back home to the German-side of Poland. By February 1940, the Red Army sealed this border, thus eliminating any chance in the future for Jews and others to seek refuge and safety. The Bug River is not too far away from Lukow, approximately 70 miles to the east of it. But Eta's family decided to stay put and stay together in Lukow, the home that was most familiar and comforting to them.

The Realities and Choices
for Jews Under Nazi Occupation

Eta's father certainly sensed the danger that lay ahead for Jews under the occupation of Nazi Germany. He was not alone among Jews in Poland and elsewhere in Nazi-occupied Europe in having this foreboding sense of doom. But to think that the Chait family and Jews overall had viable choices to deal with the threatening and deadly situation to come greatly overlooks and oversimplifies the realities they faced as the 1940s rolled ahead, especially in Poland. Here are a few major factors to consider in understanding the realities of the situation Jews faced:

First factor—the situation was beyond belief. As 1940 began, no one would have believed that in just a few years the Nazis' systematic policy of confinement of Jews into ghettos followed by mass murder in death camps and elsewhere would happen. Even Eta's father, who knew the situation was bleak, never talked about expecting mass murder to arrive. At the start of 1940, World War II had mainly been limited to Poland, where the Chait family lived. There was no sense for anyone, Jew and non-Jew alike, to know that within two years, Germany, with other allies to help, would conquer most of Europe and subsequently have the territorial control to unleash the full horrors of the Holocaust from there. Of course, on top of all this, the Nazis were masters of propaganda. Their brutal and murderous intentions were not being broadcasted directly to the world. The predominant message to the masses of people was that Jews were being sent off to work camps for a better life. Thus, for many Jewish families including Eta's family, even while suffering in the confinement of ghettos, their best option was hope. Hope that one day this craziness would pass. Hope that one day soon the Allied forces would defeat Germany.

A second factor—Jews as a minority were up against impossible odds. Reinforcements were not coming to help the persecuted Jews. There was no army that came to defend and rescue the oppressed. Before the Holocaust began, Jews were a small minority of the population living throughout the countries of Europe, citizens merely trying to lead peaceful lives. Some Jews, like Eta's father and two of her brothers, served within the armed forces of the countries in which they lived. But once defeated and conquered by Germany, their life as a soldier ended. They were ordinary citizens. Jews were not a single country with its own defense forces trained and equipped to fight against this powerful enemy. Nazi Germany, on the other hand, had at its disposal millions to fight in its military and serve in its police and security units to enforce its murderous policies. It also had massive weaponry and the full force of a government behind its actions. Jews had none of these resources nor any legal support. Plus, in most countries Germany conquered throughout Europe, local law enforcement and others were enlisted to join in the roundup, persecution, and murder of Jews. These local collaborators helped increase Germany's grip and control over the Jews. How could Eta or any other Jew think that armed resistance was an option to consider against these impossible odds?

A third major factor—indifference from world leaders. Jews, as "the others," did not have public opinion or support from other governments in the world. Even when news began to leak to leaders of Allied governments by the end of 1942 about the death camps and murderous tactics of Hitler and his regime, expressing indignation, and taking action to help were not on the agenda. The emphasis voiced by President Franklin Roosevelt of the United States and Prime Minister Winston Churchill of Great Britain was that winning the war—not rescuing Jews facing murder—was the main priority and best way to go. The reports on what was happening in the death camps were hard for anyone to believe anyway. So even if a Jew thought fighting might be a viable option to take against this Nazi scourge, despite the essentially impossible odds to ever succeed and stay alive, one was on his own. Again, no military supplies nor major force was coming to help. At least Tateh and Eta held no false expectations that a greater power was coming to help. They knew that surviving, let alone resisting in any way, was up to them.

A fourth major factor—the bystanders. This was the mass citizenry of non-Jews who chose to look the other way. Instilling fear helped many stay away from getting involved to resist and help. In the many European countries Germany occupied, it passed laws that made helping Jews and other people the Nazis labeled as "undesirables" illegal with severe consequences if one broke the law. In Poland, the most severe consequences were utilized against those non-Jews who attempted to help Jews. Often the person was murdered on the spot. Then as an example, they hung the body up in the neighborhood for everyone else to see. This was the Nazi way to send a message to the rest of the people in the area.

Beyond the fear this terror created, the vast majority of locals in the Nazi-occupied countries were not interested in helping anyway; indifference ruled the day. Life was tough enough under the conditions of wartime to care about others in dire need. On top of this, Jews who got away from the Nazi clutches often faced locals filled with hostility and anti-Semitism against them. In particular, Poland had the largest underground resistance group known as the Polish Home Army. Many of its factions put as much if not more energy into attacking Jews they encountered as they did into resisting the German occupiers of their country. Eta would later learn that this Polish resistance group would end up being the biggest enemy to contend with in her partisan life. Yet, amazingly, she would still be able to find some local Poles (Catholics), who would provide some form of assistance.

Therefore, even if one was fortunate enough to escape a Nazi-controlled ghetto alive, where would that person go? There were no inns and lodges with plenty of food on hand, waiting to offer places of safe refuge for Jews in Europe. What faced Jews who made it into the woods of Poland and Eastern Europe was living outdoors with no handy shelter and no reliable source of food. When the cold, harsh conditions of winter inevitably came, surviving the elements was often as difficult as surviving the hostile oppressor.

Then, on top of these hostile and harsh conditions, even if a Jew was inclined to join the resistance, a major obstacle that stopped the person was family. Leaving family is never easy to do. Yet, grandparents generally do not make good resistance fighters nor do they have much interest in joining up. Neither do young children. Even if one was a young and able-bodied person willing to go off and fight, what does he or she do with parents and younger siblings? Or, if one was a young adult parent with small children, who looks after their children if the person decides to join a partisan unit? Additionally, how many middle-aged to elderly parents would want to see their teenage or young adult children leave to fight in an impossibly hard and likely suicidal fight?

For many Jewish families, their best hope (they thought) was to stay together and try to survive the horrors that faced them. It was a common-sense strategy that Eta, her family, and most Jews held. The emotional pain of parents separating from a young child or for a young adult separating from a parent or other loved ones was too hard to overcome, especially when it meant going out into a dangerous, unknown world. The strong bond of love, that families have, like that of Eta and her family, made resistance not at all a viable option. Not separating from family, especially in her older brother Schulem's case, would in hindsight fill Eta with regrets later on in life.

Eta Moves Toward Resistance

Yet despite these harsh realities Jews faced, especially in Poland, Eta's fighting spirit led her down a path of resistance early on when the Nazis conquered her home country. As the Chait family was now settled back in Lukow; by the end of November 1939, Eta decided it was soon time to go back to Lodz and bring back a few guns she knew were hidden there. For a couple of months, while still living in Lodz, Eta had stepped in to help run a downtown restaurant in that city. Its Jewish owners had abandoned their involvement with the restaurant when the Germans showed up in September. Since people did not think Eta was Jewish, and she did not reveal otherwise, she stepped in for the former owners to help run the business.

Eta learned from the chef there, whose name she knew as Janek, how to steal guns from the Germans. As German army officers started frequenting the restaurant, they would hang their coats on a coat rack by the basement door with their holsters and handguns and even rifles on occasion underneath their overcoats. Janek, eventually with Eta's help, would sneak downstairs in the restaurant and steal the guns away from the rack, leaving the coats and holsters where they were. He then hid the weapons in a cellar under the restaurant. Over the course of a month, eleven weapons were confiscated this way. Janek banked on the officers not reporting that they had lost their guns for fear of humiliation and punishment they would likely encounter from their superiors. The officers never questioned any of the staff in the restaurant when they walked away empty handed after a good meal and a few drinks. Likely they did not realize anything was missing until they were well gone from the restaurant.

Janek gave Eta his address in Lodz just before she was to leave to return to Lukow. He told her that he had hidden the guns at his house and that he would keep one for himself, but she could have the rest when she was ready to come get them. Over the course of a few weeks, in late 1939 and early 1940, Eta was ready to act. She made three trips by train from Lukow to Lodz and back retrieving six pistols and two rifles from Janek's home. Gathering eight guns was a good haul considering the high risk involved in the trips. When she went out in public and on her trips to get the weapons, Eta did not wear the Jewish star on her clothing—an offense that would lead to arrest and possible execution if caught by the SS or its police arm, the Gestapo. Posing as a Christian, she would instead wear the crucifix she had been given by her friend Lola's mother. Perilously for her, she did not have the identification papers that Poles were now being required to carry. She brought large handbags and in one case a duffle bag, packed with woman's clothing in which to hide the guns, while transporting them back home. If she had been asked to show her papers, which she did not have, that would have created suspicion and likely an inspection of what was in her bags. One such check and she'd be gone.

On the last of the trips home, with a couple of pistols in her handbag, Gestapo officers appeared on the train and started walking through to check people's identification papers. Tension filled Eta. Sitting across from her was a nun. She must have seen the scared look on Eta's face. As the train was pulling in to a station for one of its stops, the nun stood up and ordered Eta to come with her as if she were her servant. "Time to depart. Get my suitcase and your things and come along." Eta nodded her head and stood up. Acting like a servant, she complied by grabbing the nun's suitcase and her own bag too. She followed the nun out of the train past the Nazi police officers, keeping her head down the whole way so as not to make any eye contact. The nun had Eta walk with her for a couple of blocks. No words were spoken between them. Eta just looked straight ahead and kept walking beside this nun, someone she had never met before. Then the nun stopped and blessed Eta to stay safe and well and sent Eta on her way. Eta softly replied, "Thank you, sister," and departed.

Whether the nun knew what Eta was up to or if she was Jewish, and it was possible that she knew both points, her quick actions saved Eta from serious trouble. Eta was able to catch a later train, one that was quiet with no Gestapo on it, and make it back home safely to Lukow with her contraband.

At the same time, as the Chait family was settling back to life in Lukow, Eta's father resumed his old trade—baking bread and rolls to help feed poor Jews and supply restaurants as he used to do. For Jews in particular, food was becoming harder to come by under Nazi rule. He did this baking quietly in their basement. His actions were now considered illegal by the Nazi authorities. No Jew was allowed to start up any kind of business or service.

As Eta was finishing up her gun-smuggling venture, a restless Schulem was about to act on his own fighting spirit too. Sticking around the house was not what he wanted to be doing, even if that was the best course for his own safety. As a young man in his mid-20s, he was a prime target for the Germans to capture and be thrown into forced labor. If the Germans were to find out that he had been a soldier in the Polish army, the consequences of being caught could even be worse. So Schulem, while antsy, was laying low.

One day he decided to go for a walk along the Jata River, the main river that runs through the town of Lukow. He came upon two German soldiers who yelled at him to stop. They then attempted to physically apprehend him. Boy, were they in for a surprise. Instead of running, Schulem stood his ground and punched them both, one in the stomach and the other under his chin. Schulem's quick and strong blows left them stunned and hurting. He knocked their heads together and pushed the two soldiers into the river. Then, Schulem took their rifles and quickly ran away. He hid the weapons in an orchard grove near the Chait home and told Eta about it. She was quite pleased to hear what her tough brother, Schulem, had done. Fortunately, no German forces came looking for Schulem afterwards. Likely the two soldiers were too embarrassed to tell their superiors what had happened to them at the hands of one single Jew.

At the same time, Tateh was quietly having meetings with one of the Jewish community leaders of Lukow—Moishe Weintraub. Weintraub had established himself with the Nazi authorities as the point person for dealing with the local Jewish community, which is what the authorities wanted. However, unbeknownst to them, he was also serving as one of the leaders of Jewish underground activities. Through Mr. Weintraub's position, and at Tateh's urging, Eta got a job as a clerk with the Arbeitsamp, the German employment agency. Through this work center, assignments would come for Jews and non-Jewish Poles to go into labor detachments the Germans required, even off to Germany as forced labor. Eta's job was to process all the paperwork that came with this.

Tateh's message to Eta was to do whatever she could to help as many people as she could in any way that she could, and not let the potential of danger stop her. His confidence and belief in his daughter's will and spirit, along with the Chait family's principle of service to others, was under the most extreme and difficult circumstances now being called upon as an undertaking for Eta. Eta's mother, Mammushe, was not initially aware of the job Eta took on with her father's encouragement, let alone the gun smuggling she had done. These were not activities she would have wanted for her daughter to get mixed up with. She was not pleased at all when she learned a little later about Eta's involvement at the German work agency. With her father's support, Eta nevertheless continued in this job.

As desperate people came to see Eta at her work in the offices of the Arbeitsamp, quietly pleading for themselves or for their son or daughter not to be sent off into forced labor, she started to get creative by falsifying records. She would write in various conditions on the forms—such as medical issues or already having an important job—that would excuse people from these dreaded labor assignments. In one case, for a man named Avrum, known as the thief of Lukow, she had put on the record that he was an important chauffeur. He was later apprehended one night by the Gestapo for loitering out on the streets. When the Gestapo agents questioned Eta about what this man's registered job was and why he would be walking the streets at night, she quickly and convincingly explained that chauffeur was his actual job and that he sometimes did emergency driving at night. Avrum was released. Eta's calm and confident manner came through for her again.

Eta's fluency in German also played a vital role. She volunteered to help clean the offices in the work center. She sometimes would go in to do the cleaning while the Gestapo officers were holding their meetings, who ignored her as just some Polish cleaning lady. She would pick up intelligence this way to share with her father and Mr. Weintraub. Importantly, she learned about the Nazis imminent plan to soon create a Judenrat, the Jewish Council, and a police force with it designed to manage all Jewish affairs in Lukow. She also heard talk among these officers about concentration camps soon to be established where Jews and other undesirables would go to and never return.

By mid-1940, Eta had been at her job as a clerk at the work center for nearly six months. She had been taking a significant risk with her spying and with her creative ways of filling out work forms within the German administrative bureaucracy. But how long could these high-risk efforts continue undetected?

6

*S*truggles and Loss

Through the middle of 1940, Eta and her family were doing as well as could be expected under the most difficult of circumstances. Under the noses of the Nazi authorities, Eta's father was maintaining a bakery business which was helping support his family and feed fellow Jews. Everyone in the family was together in Lukow. And Eta was carrying on her clandestine activities, doing whatever she could to help others as her father greatly encouraged.

But these making-the-best-of bad times would soon change. Eta would soon enter into one of the darkest periods of her life over the next nearly three years, coinciding with what happened to Jews in Poland and elsewhere in Eastern Europe. The "worst of times" was right around the corner.

Nazi Ghettoization of Poland

In February 1940, Lodz became the first major city in Nazi-occupied Poland to confine Jews into a small section of the city, fence them in, and have the entrance points guarded with SS forces. These confined spaces were called ghettos and were formed throughout Nazi-occupied Poland during the rest of the year and into the spring of 1941, with the largest ghettos in such cities as Lublin, Bialystok, Krakow, Radom, Lvov, and, of course,

Warsaw. The capital city of the former country of Poland had the biggest ghetto—approximately a half million Jews put into a space of a little less than two square miles. In a relatively short time, the many ghettos of various sizes throughout the occupied land became bastions for starvation, disease, and periodic acts of brutality and murder by the SS.

As 1940 moved forward, an open ghetto existed in the town of Lukow. Jews were ordered to move into the main section where the majority had lived prior to the occupation. Signs were erected as to where the borders of this ghetto were, but no fencing and barbed wire were installed to hem people in. Jews who would try to venture beyond these boundaries without German authorization were still in high danger if caught by the authorities. Jews were already ordered to have the yellow star or blue armband on their clothing when out in public, and were severely punished and sent away if caught without either. So venturing outside of this open ghetto was not a feasible option to pursue. Eta and her family already lived in this section, crowded into their apartment, so there was little change for them. They were okay for the time being.

But the Jewish ghetto in Lukow was becoming even more crowded. By the end of 1939, 2,500 Jews from elsewhere in Poland had been moved into Lukow. This number also included some Jews from the now-Nazi Germany ally of Slovakia, once part of the country of Czechoslovakia. Throughout 1940, more Jews would be moved into Lukow from different areas of Poland and from other countries in Europe. In time, Lukow would be required to accommodate more than double the population of Jews compared to what it was prior to the start of the war.

Nazi Grip Forms Throughout Europe

By July 1940, the countries of northern and western Europe who had come under attack from the military forces of Nazi Germany during the spring had surrendered and were now taken over. This included Norway, Denmark, The Netherlands, Luxembourg, Belgium, and mighty France. Great Britain, bombed and battered, was still standing but totally on its own in Europe against Hitler's onslaught. The United States, in its isolationist mode, was still sitting out this war. Help was not coming for the Jews trapped in Poland. At the same time, the Soviet Union had established its control, as part of its non-aggression pact with Germany, not only over the eastern zone of Poland but also the rest of Eastern Europe as well—the Baltic States, Ukraine, and Byelorussia.

Then came June 22, 1941. Viewing that the timing was right and as was intended all along, Hitler ordered German military forces to attack the Soviet Union. The time had come to put an end to the Communist scourge. The Red Army was ill prepared for this major German offensive. Within six months, the whole eastern sphere of Europe that had been under the occupation of the Soviet Union plus much of the country's Russian province itself had been overwhelmed by German forces. German forces by the end of 1941 were within 20 miles of the capital of Moscow. Jews in these newly-occupied areas, some who had fled Poland almost a couple of years before, were now trapped. More ghettos were formed to confine and terrorize them. But first came a measure of ethnic cleansing. In the last six months of 1941, as German forces were conquering Poland through Eastern Europe, the SS-operated Einsatzgruppen, murder squads, were sent in right afterwards to these newly-occupied territories. Comprised not only of Germans, they contained men from Romania and Lithuania who were enlisted to help. Before 1941 was over, more than a million-and-a-half people from these conquered areas had been lined up and shot to death. The vast majority were Jews.

As 1942 forged ahead, Poland was a land dotted with a multitude of concentration camps and labor camps. Even more horrific, the six main death camps that manufactured murder with their gas chambers were soon up and running: Auschwitz-Birkenau, Sobibor, Chelmno, Belzec, Majdanek, and Treblinka. By mid-summer 1942, Jews from Poland and ghettos elsewhere across Europe were being deported continuously by cattle car trains to these death camps in Poland. Treblinka would be where Jews from Lukow would be sent for their final destination.

Struggles Ahead For Eta and Her Family

Rewinding back to mid-1940, the struggles were just beginning for Eta and her family. Around this time, Mr. Weintraub was somehow betrayed, leading to his arrest by the SS along with a few associates in his budding underground group. They and their families were hauled away from Lukow and never seen again.

Another betrayal of unknown origin during the summer of 1940 led to a few Gestapo officers showing up unexpectedly one day at Eta's father's bakery. As mentioned before, having your own business was now illegal for Jews in Poland. Tateh dressed in his bakery apron as he was confronted by the Gestapo, had been discovered. Then one of the police officers punched Tateh in the face while yelling at him that it was illegal for Jews to have such unauthorized enterprises. Eta was there at the time. Something inside her sparked and propelled her to yell back at the German officers. "There is no reason to hit my father! Whatever business you need to do here, do so professionally." All the startled Gestapo officers on hand went silent and did not raise a hand again to anyone present. Instead of destroying the bakery, one of the officers softly announced that this man, a local Pole who was with them, would now be running this business. The Polish man, who knew her father, quietly whispered to Eta that if she and her family needed any food, he would be there to help them. But Tateh was being arrested and taken away. Eta was so disturbed, and she would not sit back quietly.

A short time after her father's arrest, Eta went downtown to a cafe frequented by the Gestapo chief in Lukow. He was there having his lunch when she entered. She went directly to his table, sat down, and pulled away the scarf blocking the yellow star on her clothing to reveal she was a Jew. In perfect German, she firmly recounted to the police chief about the misconduct of one of his officers in arresting her father, who was merely a good man taking care of his family, and insisted that he should be released to come home to his family. The chief smiled a bit and nodded his head, likely impressed by the way Eta presented herself. He then called over two Gestapo officers sitting at a nearby table. He wrote out an order and gave it to them. Before the day was over, Eta was escorting her father back home.

But in the German employment agency in which Eta worked, suspicion was growing from her superiors about what she was really doing in her job as a clerk. A young German Jewish woman was brought in to work alongside Eta, serving as a spy and watching how she was filling out the work forms. The non-Jewish Poles who worked in this office knew and respected Eta and always pretended that they did not know anything was amiss. But this young woman, who happened to be Jewish, would periodically be staring at Eta as she did her paperwork. Eta noticed this but tried not to give it much thought. Sure enough, the girl betrayed Eta, secretly reporting Eta's suspicious activities to the German authorities. In July 1940, Gestapo agents came one day to the work center and arrested Eta. She would hear later that the Jewish girl who betrayed her, when being pulled away in a German roundup, spoke up about how she had been so helpful to the Nazis. The Gestapo men scoffed at her. This girl after all was a Jew. She was shot dead on the spot.

Eta then went through harsh interrogation. Apparently not certain that she was Jewish, the rough questioning focused not only on what group she was working with but also whether she was a Jew. When she was brought to the first prison in Radzyn, the nearest city to Lukow, which was less than 20 miles away, she was greeted in the interrogation room by two attack dogs that had blood on their mouths from mauling other prisoners. Instead of being frightened, Eta merely reached out and started hugging the dogs as if they were cute puppies. Both dogs then started wagging their tails and licking her.

A short time later she was transferred to a prison in Lublin, the major city in the country's south. Upon arrival, the brutal interrogations by the SS continued. Beyond being yelled at and threatened, she suffered through beatings—including having a billy club taken to her back and legs. Eta said little and didn't give anyone up in all the interrogations. What responses she gave were kept short and spoken in perfect German.

At this Lublin prison, which was a former castle, Eta was then placed in a large cell with other women, all non-Jewish, who were common criminals or political prisoners. She may have been the only Jew in the whole prison, as everyone she came across or heard about was Christian. She started organizing seminar groups each day to share stories from her reading interests and to do something positive to pull the Polish women together. In time, these daily group sessions found all the women attending and happily participating.

One woman in particular in this cell tended to look after Eta. She was known as a madam and had been arrested for running a house of prostitution. Periodically Eta received care packages of food from her mother, although she did not know at the time who they were from. The two sons of this madam were the ones who brought in the packages, and the madam would then pass on the packages to Eta with a smile. Eta would share what she could with her cellmates. She would eventually learn that this madam was the prostitute Eta had befriended some ten years prior with friendly conversation and books from the library when she would come in to her father's bakery.

One day in late May 1941, nearly 11 months after she had been arrested, Eta was called out of her cell by one of the Polish guards. She was uncertain why she had been called to come out and wondered if she was in for a rough interrogation. The guard then escorted her out of the prison to a truck waiting there for her. Two young men by the truck asked her to quickly put on a flowered dress and pin a flower in her hair, giving her a similar appearance to the other "ladies of the night" sitting inside the truck. Eta, realizing that this looked like a chance to get out of prison, went along and changed into the outfit. Other than a quick comment by one of the young men, "You'll be fine. Please get in the back of the truck," nothing else was said. Eta quickly jumped in the truck and rode along inside with the other ladies. Little was spoken other than a few giggles every now and then by a few of the ladies dressed like her.

To her surprise, a few hours later, Eta was dropped off back home in Lukow. The two young men who helped her escape were the madam's two sons. As Eta found out later, the madam's two sons had been in touch with her parents periodically at the urging of their mother. Mammushe, Eta's mother, was in support of the escape plan, having sold all the family's jewelry that then served as a bribe for the Polish prison guard. The madam's two sons orchestrated the whole risky venture. Mammushe was, of course, ecstatic to see Eta home safely. She had slept on the floor the whole time her eldest daughter had been taken away to prison, almost a full year, praying that she would see her again one day.

Eta laid low in the family's house for a little while, and fortunately no one from the authorities came looking for her. For all the adversity and torture she had been through, Eta nevertheless came out strong and fit and maintained a steady and sturdy 125 pounds on her five foot-three-inch frame.

Terror Comes To Lukow

In the meantime, Jews continued to come into Lukow from other parts of Poland and Europe. The ghetto grew more crowded. Food for many became harder to come by. The Chait family no longer had their apartment to themselves. They had a family of six, two parents with four children, all inside their apartment now. Eta's father and her brothers Schulem and Moishe were able to get work assignments at a lumber yard on the outskirts of Lukow. Eta was able to get a job at a poultry plant owned and managed by a Mr. Dietz.

As 1941 came to a close, beyond the increasingly tough conditions for Jews in Lukow, violence from the Nazis started to intensify. In December 1941, Commander Fischer of the SS in charge of the Radzyn district, which included Lukow, ordered all Jews to turn in their furs. Those handful of Jews who owned such valuable items and tried to keep them concealed were found out. All were executed.

By May 1942, the ghetto in Lukow now numbered over 10,000 Jews. In mid-September 1942, the ghetto was sealed with barbed wire fencing to keep in all the Jews. The ghetto now numbered around 15,000 Jews, well more than twice the town's Jewish population prior to the Nazi occupation.

On October 5, 1942, the first main action in Lukow targeting Jews, or aktion in German as it was called, was under way. The roundup of Jews from the ghetto for deportation them to the Treblinka death camp in Poland had begun. German SS units with the help of Ukranian police and the blue police, the local Polish law enforcement units dressed in their blue uniforms, swooped in. Four thousand of the Jews who had been ordered to come to the town's central market just outside the ghetto were pushed, prodded, and boarded onto the crowded train (cattle cars just waiting there) at the nearby station. They were then shipped away on the train, not knowing where they were headed. Another 500 Jews were driven outside of town in the back of trucks into nearby woods. They were shot to death by an execution squad, the last rabbi of the community among them. At the time of this roundup, Eta was away from home. She had been running an errand for Mr. Dietz and was on her way to the train station to pick up a package for him.

As she was getting close to the train station, three young men, Polish Catholic brothers who knew Eta, saw her from the restaurant they were in as she came walking by at just the wrong time. They quickly stepped out of the restaurant and pulled her in. They put an apron on her and had her work in the kitchen until the aktion finally ended that day. Eta knew what was happening outside but kept herself busy in the restaurant so as not to see. She had been spared for the time being.

Over the next month, a few more raids and roundups occurred in the Lukow ghetto that resulted in another 4,000 plus Jews getting deported to Treblinka and a few hundred more executed, this time in front of the town's courthouse and at the Jewish cemetery. After the October 5th raid, many Jews in the ghetto were desperately seeking to hide, in attics or cellars or wherever they might avoid discovery. Nazi propaganda was aimed to lure them out, by making announcements that told the Jews to come to the central market to get new identification cards. Such ID's would come with food and no deportation.

Those who did not buy into this false propaganda were still getting captured in violent raids by the SS coming into the ghetto with the local police helping them. Come November 1942, Eta's family would be hit.

While her father and two brothers, Schulem and Moishe, were away working at the lumberyard outside of town, Eta was home with the rest of her family. As the Nazi aktion force came roaring into Lukow, a few thousand Jews began to congregate in the central market as ordered by the SS, including Eta and her family members who had been at home at the time. Amidst the chaos and panic, Eta's sister Mara, married and now eight months pregnant, was calling out looking for her husband. An SS guard was standing nearby, heard her calls. He then turned, walked over to Mara, and mercilessly proceeded to use the butt of his rifle on her. He repeatedly hit her in her pregnant stomach. With a stone-cold look on his face, he kept hitting her until she was beaten to death. As this horror was happening, Eta hugged her mother tightly and shielded her eyes from this brutal horror, softly saying amidst her mother's tears, "Don't look out, look at me." Then when Mara's husband came frantically running from a distance, another SS policeman nearby pulled out his pistol. He shot Mara's husband to death right next to where her limp body laid on the ground.

Mr. Dietz bravely came into the market as this chaos and terror was happening. He had his list of Jewish workers, calling for them to be released so they could get back to work at his poultry plant. Eta did not want to leave her family. But then her sister, Faige, age 15 and 11 years younger than Eta, took off her sweater and gave it to Eta. Faige sternly then said to Eta, "I will look after Mammushe and our younger brothers and sisters." She paused and Eta was still standing there almost frozen. "Go! Get back to work where you belong," Faige added, as she started to push Eta away to join Mr. Dietz. Just then another man came walking through the market. He came up to Eta and gave her a kiss on the lips. He then took her by the arm and had her start walking forward with him. He was smiling the whole time, as if they were two lovers going for a stroll down the street. This man was the town pimp, whose girlfriend was the young prostitute Eta once befriended—now the madam who helped her escape from prison. As a result of this ruse, Eta was able to then join Mr. Dietz and get away from this latest roundup.

A short time after this terrifying roundup occurred in the market, the Nazis raided the lumberyard outside of town where Eta's father and her two brothers worked. The business was shut down and all the Jews in it were beaten and taken away for deportation. A few nights later while Eta was working at the Dietz poultry plant where she also slept sometimes, she saw Tateh, Schulem, and Moishe waiting outside. Her father and older brother had bruises on their faces while her younger brother was in severe pain with a separated shoulder. They had all managed to jump off the deportation train and make their way back to Lukow. Eta asked a friend she worked with at the plant who had been a medical student to come and help. He was able to pop Moishe's shoulder back in to place, easing his pain greatly. Eta then hid her three family members for a few days in a lumber shed at the factory.

By mid-November 1942, the raids found Lukow with an estimated 4,000 Jews remaining in its ghetto. Since their apartment had been raided previously and their hiding place there found out, Eta, Tateh, Schulem, Moishe, and Faige were able to take residence in an old bakery by the front gate of the ghetto. Cots had been pulled into the place, now crowded with two dozen plus Jews in it.

Faige, amidst the chaos of the recent raid, had been pushed away by Mammushe and was able to run away and make it back to the family. Eta was very distraught. Her sister Mara, pregnant with her family's first grandchild, was dead. Her mother and five youngest siblings had all been hauled away. She knew that she likely would never see them again.

At some point before the end of the year of 1942, a 17-year old Jewish boy looking to sneak in to the Dietz plant to see his mother saw a German guard outside. In his rage over what happened to the Jews of Lukow, the teen shot the guard dead. When word soon reached the Nazi authorities, they swooped down on the plant, executing the Jewish men there and closing Mr. Dietz's factory forever. The non-Jewish Poles were now out of work too, and Eta and the other Jewish women at the plant returned to reside in the ghetto.

Eta's family got by. To help feed her family, Eta was paid in food by Polish families who she wrote letters of appeal for in an effort to get their family members returned home—loved ones who had been sent away into forced labor. In addition, the man who took over Tateh's bakery sometimes came by and provided food. But everyone waited and wondered what might come next. Then on May 2, 1943, the Nazis launched the final liquidation of the ghetto in Lukow.

The time had come to deport the remaining Jews of Lukow to the Treblinka death camp. As the German force moved in to carry out the final liquidation, the Lukow ghetto was set on fire. Smoke was everywhere. As the roundup was in full force, Eta and her father were standing near each other on the edge of the central market close by the entrance to the ghetto. At a distance, she could see her brother Schulem at the far end deep inside the ghetto. Moishe and Faige were scattered about and could not be seen amidst all the panic. But soon her view of Schulem was lost in all the smoke. Eta and Tateh seized the opportunity and ran unseen out of the market to the house next to where they had been staying. They climbed a ladder that took them into an attic and then pushed the ladder away.

The final liquidation took place over the course of three days, with the Nazis torching much of the ghetto. Most of the remaining Jews in Lukow had either been shot to death or put on deportation trains. This time Schulem did not jump off the train. Believing his brother and sister were in other train cars, as likely they were, there was no way he would try to escape and leave his family behind. And there was no one on the train to push him and tell him to jump off the train. Schulem would have made a great resistance fighter.

Eta and her father waited quietly while hidden in the attic, lying next to each other for four days with nothing to eat. But what lay ahead for them? Did they have a future? And anyway, was life still worth living?

Eta's father in 1943. Life in the ghetto and the deportation of most of his family by the Nazis had taken a heavy toll on him.

Dr. Leon Kiernicki, the helpful doctor of Lukow, especially for Eta and her partisan life.

Eta Chait in her mid 20s. The life as a resistance leader
and partisan in the woods was soon to begin.

Heniek Wrobel as a Polish soldier in the Soviet Red Army, 1941.
In late 1939 he was able to get out of the Nazi-occupied zone of
Poland into the Soviet zone before this possibility was closed down.

Yidl and Lola Woland's wedding picture in Poland, October 1945. Not
long before this, Yidl was an active partisan in the woods with Eta Chait.

Chana and Chaim Grinbaum at their wedding in Florence, Italy, 1946.
They first met in Florence at a DP (displaced persons) camp. Not long
before this Chaim was an active partisan in the woods with Eta Chait.

Liberation had finally come. Heniek and Eta Wrobel
were now newlyweds, still in Poland, 1945.

A memorial today in the town of Lukow for the Jews that once
were. It's on the edge of the forest by the town where Nazi
shootings of Jews occurred. (*Courtesy of Krzysztof Czubaszek*)

7

*T*he Beginning of Partisan Life

E ta did not wait until the final liquidation of the Lukow ghetto to get prepared to go into the woods and become a partisan, a resistance fighter. Two events shaped her destiny.

Preliminary Moves to Becoming a Partisan

First, she met Dr. Leon Kiernicki. He was born and raised in the Ukraine and came to Lukow in 1920 at the age of 35 to become one of its doctors. There were only six doctors working in Lukow when he started his medical practice there. He was considered a kind and considerate man whose objective was to provide quality health care to all the residents of Lukow and make it accessible to them.

When the Nazi occupation came to Lukow and the ghetto was formed, unlike most non-Jews, he continued to serve Jews. He would put on the armband as Jews were required to do and go inside the ghetto to treat the sick and injured Jews there. Sometimes his wife Maria would accompany him to help out. His giving of aid would include helping Eta Chait. In early spring 1943, she contracted typhus—a disease which sometimes led to death. He knew what medication to provide and gave

Eta a shot of it, curing her soon after. Eating again never felt so good to her.

In addition, Dr. Kiernicki started teaching Eta the skills to be a medic. She found him to be an easy man to visit and work with. While the words were never said out loud, he was actually preparing Eta with medical skills to survive and help others should she escape into the woods.

The plan to do so was underway now as well. In March 1943, Eta started talking individually to some of the young Jewish men in the ghetto about her plan. These were men in their late teens and 20s like her—she was now nearly 27—whom she knew from the various sports club activities she had been actively involved in prior to the war in the 1930s. The plan—escape from the ghetto and become partisans in the woods.

The area outside of the town of Lukow was surrounded by thick forests. It was called the Podlasie, meaning under the woods, with forests stretching to the south all the way to the city of Lublin nearly 60 miles away.

Eta started to confide in the members of this newly-formed underground group. She shared with them where she had hidden rifles—outside the ghetto in orchards—and what her ideas were for escape into the woods. In one of these secret meetings, she shared her plan, "Our best chance is to have a small number of individuals from the group sneak out of the ghetto and scout out the woods for the best place to set up a partisan camp. You might even find other Jews already in the woods we could team up with and form a partisan unit. As part of this scouting effort, you first go and retrieve the hidden rifles. That way you are ready to be part of a partisan group. Then the idea would be for you to come back and guide the rest of the Jews from our group out of the ghetto and safely into the woods to the camp you have established." Eta paused and then added, "We need to carry out this plan soon, before it is too late."

There was a sense that Eta had, and the others as well, that the final liquidation of the ghetto by the Nazis was coming soon. Everyone in the meeting voiced agreement with Eta's plan. They were anxious to execute this plan shortly.

At the same time, the scouting mission into the woods had to be done very carefully. The scuttlebutt was that the AK (the Armia Krajowa), known in English as the Polish Home Army, might have a presence in some parts of these woods. The AK was the largest of the handful of Polish resistance groups that formed during Germany's occupation of Poland. Numbering more than a quarter million fighters at its height and aligned with the Polish government-in-exile located now in London, many factions of the AK were known to be anti-Semitic and would be just as happy to hunt down Jews as they would be to attack the German occupiers.

By late April 1943, the underground group was ready to make its move and go forward with the plan. Five young men referred to as Samuel, Solomon, Marcus, Lemel, and Efrayim had been selected to serve as this initial scouting party. They snuck out of the ghetto at night. Accompanying them was a little older and now widowed woman named Raizel, sent to help cook and do laundry. Everyone in this underground group hoped their mission would succeed and that someone from the scouting party would soon return to guide the rest of the members out of the ghetto and into the woods.

However, within a week of the escape, on May 2, 1943, the final liquidation of the Lukow ghetto came. The Nazi SS forces with Ukranian guards enlisted to help surrounded the ghetto and herded the Jews into the central market. As mentioned in the previous chapter, amidst the panic and chaos of the roundup, Eta's remaining siblings, Schulem, Moshe, and Faige, were swept up and boarded onto the deportation trains. Eta and her father were able to make their way up a ladder into an attic inside a house on the edge of the ghetto as a refuge for hiding. Tateh had kicked away the ladder so nothing about this hiding place could be easily noticed. Gun shots and screams in the streets could be heard. Many of the buildings inside the ghetto were set on fire. After four days of hiding in this attic with no food or water, silence and smoke filled the night air. Much of the ghetto had been burned down and no Jew was seemingly left alive.

Escaping Away From Luke

Eta and her father came out from their hiding place and peered out its window. With no ladder to use to guide their way down, Eta just jumped, probably from a height ten feet off the ground. No problem for this young athletic woman. She landed on her feet, just like a gymnast at the end of a competitive performance who nailed a beautiful landing. In reflections in later years, Eta would recall how fear was a great motivator that helped her perform sometimes amazing physical feats. Tateh's jump from the attic was more of a fall, but he was not injured and Eta was there to help break his fall.

Despite the fear and trepidation of the unknown dangers ahead, Eta now felt a rush of excitement as if freedom was possible. Clinging to one another, Eta and her father then hurried out of Lukow and within a mile came to a pond. They went sprawling to the ground, putting their faces right into the water and drinking as much as they could. No thought entered their minds as to whether this water was clean and safe for drinking.

They then rested at a nearby tree when suddenly out of the corner of Eta's eye she saw a Polish man behind them with a shovel. This was someone on the hunt for escaped Jews, who was about to hit Tateh in the head with the shovel. Suddenly it started to rain, and Eta, in the perfect Polish she could speak, yelled out, "Holy Mother, thanks for the rain!" The startled man stopped and apologized that he almost killed them and then ran away to get out of the rain. Eta and her father quickly got up and scurried down the road, looking to move away from Lukow as fast they could. Tateh had some money in his possession and she had a gold ring. Their hope was to find a village where they could buy food.

Not long after, as the rain let up, they came upon a farmhouse. They could smell a pleasant aroma coming from the house, Eta boldly knocked on the door. A man probably in his 40s with his wife, appearing to be the same age, standing by his side opened the door. He had a look on his face that indicated he knew where they came from and why they were here. Without hesitation, he nodded his head and invited Eta and her father into the house and guided them to the kitchen table. His wife then put out milk and bread, which Eta and Tateh heartily and gratefully ate. This was their first real meal in nearly five days. When Eta offered them her ring to pay for the meal they had just been provided, the couple refused.

Eta had thusly come upon a couple that would become great allies for her partisan life ahead. Referred to as Jan and Maria Glawinski, they were a Catholic couple who did not believe in killing Jews or anyone else. Eta never knew their real names. She did not ask nor did they offer, probably safest for all involved should anyone get captured and interrogated by the authorities one day, especially by the Nazis.

The Glawinski couple had a small wooden structure behind their house, a hut where they sometimes kept rabbits. Maria suggested that Eta and her father stay in this hut for a few days to rest and recover. The Glawinski couple took out the few rabbit cages they had in the hut and provided blankets for Eta and her father to make them comfortable. Over the next few days, Jan came by to provide them with food and water. The area remained quiet; the place stayed safe.

After three days, Eta and her father had regained their strength from the good care they had received. She was ready to move on and see about finding her friends in the woods. She had informed Jan and Maria about their plans and they did not bat an eye. They could be trusted. Jan reported to Eta that a few days before she and her father had arrived, he heard about a gun battle between a group from the ghetto and some German and Polish police a few miles just south of his house on the edge of the woods. He warned her to be careful, but still thought that heading south would likely be the best direction to go in order to find her scouting group from Lukow in the woods.

Finding Their Way Into the Woods

The next morning, Eta and Tateh proceeded on foot, moving away from this welcoming farmhouse. Eta put on the gold crucifix she had been given from the mother of her Catholic friend Lola in Lodz. As she worked her way down the road, she sought information by boldly knocking on the doors of farmers' homes. Tateh would hide out in the bushes when she approached a house. Speaking Polish while wearing the crucifix, Eta was able to pass as a Catholic. Her story was that she escaped from Warsaw where her parents had been killed by the Germans for being government employees, as part of the Nazi Intelligenzaktion in the early months after Poland had been conquered in September 1939.

Over the course of the next three days, Eta and her father worked their way into the woods. In her conversations with various farmers, she wondered about any partisan activity in these parts of the woods and would slip in questions. Most were aware of such activity. While some cursed the partisans as being no-good robbers, others told her what they had seen and where and even gave her food and water, which she shared with her father.

Now about 10 days since the final liquidation of the Lukow ghetto had occurred, Eta and her father were deep into the woods. As darkness came upon them on a pleasant day in mid-May, while Eta was searching the area on her own, all of a sudden she heard a voice shouting, "Stop or I'll shoot!" She raised her hands and yelled back, "Don't worry. I am not moving anywhere." Then popping out from hiding behind a few trees with smiles on their faces came Solomon and Marcus, two members of her underground group in the ghetto. They and the others from the scouting group had made it safely into the woods and acquired the weapons Eta had secretly hidden. They were aware of the final liquidation.

Eta then gathered Tateh who had been hiding out near the main road since she went exploring in the woods. Over the next few hours, they followed the two scouts from Lukow deeper into the woods. In the wee hours before dawn, they came upon the main camp with which the scouting group had connected after escaping the ghetto.

As morning rose and everyone awakened, in front of Eta's eyes was a group of 60 Jews. They had dug bunkers into the ground as their shelter. The ratio of men to women was about two to one. Most everybody was young, late teens and early 20s. There was one older woman probably over the age of 50 as was Tateh. They were now in the woods located southeast of Lukow, approximately four to five miles away from town.

Tateh was not well. Physically he was fine and was not sick or injured. But mentally, the depression from the certain loss of his wife and nearly all of his family had been building in him. Eta had battled some of the same feelings previously as well. But since the shot from Dr. Kiernicki that cured her from typhus a couple of months prior, which coincided with her organizing an underground group in the ghetto to escape, Eta's energy and determination had driven her forward with a renewed sense of purpose and a dose of courage.

She and Tateh had made it safely into the woods. They were now part of a partisan group, an all-Jewish one at that.

8

$\mathcal{T}$he Partisan Unit Comes to Life

As the members of this newly-found partisan unit awoke that morning and came out of their two large underground bunkers where they slept, they warmly greeted the two new arrivals, Eta and her father. Eta recognized a few of the faces as being from Lukow or small villages in its vicinity. Many others were from ghettos to the south, some from as far away as the city of Lublin. What most these young Jews had in common, beyond that they had all escaped the clutches of the Nazis, was that few of them had any family members left. Some had been in the woods just a few weeks while others had escaped a few months ago. They had some weapons, much of which Eta had supplied through her scout group. They had been gathering food from local farmers near the woods and getting by in their makeshift shelter.

Eta Becomes Part of the Unit's Leadership

The group had no formal leadership structure, and no formal structure would ever get developed. However, in a short time, Eta would informally help bring leadership to the unit. The members from her Lukow scout group let it be known to the whole unit that Eta was someone that they would want involved in any strategy meeting. Her engaging, take-charge manner along with her intelligence made this easy for everyone to accept.

For the women who made it into the woods as part of partisan groups in Eastern Europe during the war, playing any kind of combatant role (one who carried a weapon and was actively involved in dangerous missions) let alone having a leadership position in these groups was quite unusual. Women, usually much fewer in number than men in these partisan units, were most commonly noncombatants. Their role was to help cook, clean, and serve in nurse-type roles to care for the sick and wounded. These were important roles that gave valuable support within partisan units. Being a combatant, and more so, even being someone who participated in strategy planning sessions and decisions for the partisan group was a role most often reserved for the men.

Within this unit, which never took on a formal name, Eta played the combatant and leadership roles as well as the doctor or medic role—skills she had acquired under the tutelage of Dr. Leon Kiernicki. As such, she was a vital contributor and leader of the group. When Eta spoke in meetings, making comments such as, "Here is a strategy we should consider using," or "I've got an idea that can help," the men listened attentively to her. Her confidence and her intelligence just pulled them in, wanting to hear what she had to say.

Soon there would evolve a core group that kept this partisan unit driving forward that Eta got to know well. They were men in their early 20s, a little younger than she was—among them Moshe Danyilak, Chaim Grinbaum, Yidl Woland, and David Rendel. They were not men tall in stature, all were under six feet in height, but they were strong, focused, and determined. Moshe, in particular, was only around five feet six inches tall but had broad shoulders and dark, curly hair. Yidl in time would be the person Eta would rely on most to organize the unit's defense activities. They all got along well, were willing to work together, and greatly respected Eta as part of the unit's informal leadership. Chaim and Yidl, besides being similar in age, now 23 in the summer of 1943, each had something else in common. Both had made their way into the woods by escaping from a deportation train that was taking Jews out of the ghettos to the Treblinka death camp, a most amazing feat.

Chaim was the second youngest of eight children. He was born and raised in Lukow. His formal education ended after 8th grade, as he was needed to work helping his father run a bakery. He learned tailoring skills from his mother, which would come in handy later in life. His family had moved to Lodz shortly after the war broke out in September 1939 and ultimately became trapped in the ghetto there. In the latter half of 1942, as the deportation of Jews out of the ghettos into the death camps was under way, Chaim actually escaped the deportation train twice.

On the first occasion, Chaim saw sunlight gleaming through the small hole in the ceiling of the cattle car in which he was locked inside. As the train moved ahead, looking up, he climbed up over people crowded in the cattle car with him, climbing on their backs and shoulders as he propelled himself upwards. A few murmurs were heard in his train car, but most people stayed quiet and watched with curiosity to see what Chaim was doing. Now reaching the near the top of the train car, with a mighty push, he was able to open the ceiling by the small hole. Without hesitation, he then jumped off the moving train, rolled around on the grass below, and quickly sprung to his feet. Chaim then started to run and got away. No shots from guards on the train were fired in his direction. He had pulled off an amazing escape without getting noticed. But Chaim did not stay away for very long. Being out on his own in the woods and terribly missing his family, he eventually walked back into the Lodz ghetto.

The second time he was rounded up and boarded on the train, Chaim did the same thing, climbing up over people and out of the ceiling of the cattle car. This time as he ran away, shots were fired in his direction. He kept running not realizing he had received a flesh wound in his buttocks. By early 1943, he had made his way into the woods outside of Lukow and was now part of this newly-formed partisan unit.

Yidl Woland was also born and raised in Lukow and knew of Eta as he was growing up there. She was four years older than him. He was one of nine children. His father worked as a butcher and wanted Yidl to become a rabbi. That was not his interest, however, as he would follow his father on the path to become a butcher.

In late 1942 or early 1943, Yidl escaped a deportation train departing the Lukow ghetto by going right out the door. Somewhere along its route the train stopped momentarily and the door to the cattle car Yidl was in opened. Yidl grabbed the night stick from the Nazi guard who opened the door, hit him hard, and jumped off the train with four young men jumping off right behind him. Shots from the guards on the train rang out immediately. Three of the young Jewish men were killed. Yidl and one other escapee kept running. Yidl was grazed in the leg but never slowed down. He and the other young man eventually hooked up with other stray Jews they found in the woods outside of Lukow, and by May 1943, welcomed Eta into their newly-formed partisan unit. Yidl was glad to have her involved.

David Rendel was also born and raised in Lukow. He was now near the age of 20 and a partisan in the woods aligned with this all-Jewish unit. Like Chaim Grinbaum and Yidl Woland, he arrived in the woods the same way. He, too, jumped off a deportation train and then kept running, eventually making his way to the woods outside of Lukow.

By June 1943 as spring rolled into summer, the partisan unit now had grown to include 80 Jews and was in active operation. The bunkers were well built, running a few feet deep under the ground with leafy tree branches and even a few stolen barn doors as their secret cover at the top. A dozen or more people could sleep snuggly in a bunker. Food missions were in full operation; sometimes runs were carried out a few times a week, usually in the evening. Chaim was one of the active unit members leading these food missions.

Outside the woods where the partisan unit resided were many little villages and farms. Before Eta joined the group, a strong relationship had been built with one such farmer who actively supplied the group with bread. Sometimes through bartering with villagers and farmers and sometimes through quiet raids at night, the partisan group was able to acquire fruits and vegetables and an occasional animal to cook. Yidl and his butchering skills came in handy when an animal was brought in. Being kosher and following its dietary laws was no longer a consideration. The group treaded carefully as it approached various farms, being on the lookout for German forces who sometimes came by to take food for their own needs from these same farmers. The group did well overall in its regular missions to seek out food. No one was starving, and eating a lot of potatoes was common.

Elizabeth Goes into Action

At the same time, Eta served the partisan unit very well, acting as Elizabeth Bryczemak, and carrying out missions mostly on her own. She had started perfecting this non-Jewish character when she first escaped the Lukow ghetto with her father back in May. With her crucifix, perfect Polish, and a backstory to match, Eta would go into the various villages within a few miles outside the woods from their partisan camp and gather food, ammunition, intelligence, and even stray Jews.

Because of the war and Nazi occupation, education for school-aged children in these rural areas was often disrupted. Eta would make money by offering her services to tutor the children in these families. With this money, she would purchase food for her partisan unit and sometimes weapons and ammunition, too. She would pay close attention to the scuttlebutt about the German arrival in a given area in order to gather food and about possible movements of the AK, the Polish Home Army resistance group. It was best to stay well out of the reach of both forces.

Eta also made a good contact with someone referred to as Stanislaw, a key member of the AL. The Armia Ludowa (AL), in English called the People's Army, was another Polish resistance group. It was smaller in number than the AK and was comprised mostly of leftists, usually socialists and communists. Many members of the AL later became part of the communist government that would take control of Poland after World War II.

Stanislaw and his AL unit in the area were not anti-Semitic. He would prove to be a helpful ally and source to Eta both with intelligence about German movements as well as those of the rival AK. He also occasionally helped supply Eta with weapons and ammunition, including materials for making bombs. He would help her obtain false identity papers to fortify her Elizabeth Bryczemak persona.

The Partisan Unit Goes on the Attack

Road 63 was the main road connecting Lukow to Radzin, which was a little less than 20 miles south of Lukow. Radzin was a major post both for German military forces as well as the SS and its police arm, the Gestapo. It even had a palace that the Germans took over as the site of their headquarters in this city. Road 63 was a central route the Germans used regularly to transport food and military supplies from the north in Poland down to Radzin. It was a perfect target to hit if done right.

As Eta learned on her missions as Elizabeth, and later shared with her partisan unit, the AK forces in their vicinity were predominantly hiding out in the woods north and west of Lukow, while her unit was in the woods south and east of Lukow. The AK also looked to sometimes carry out sabotage attacks on German convoys traveling along Road 63; so the trick was to try and not hit the same convoy along the same route, on the same day. Plus, certain German convoys carrying many soldiers would be too tall of a task to try to hit and get away with it unscathed. With this intelligence Eta had gathered that the Germans would be soon coming into their vicinity for a major food pickup, but not a major force of troops with it, the time seemed to be right to strike.

In late June or early July 1943, Yidl Woland led a small group of men and one woman, Eta, from the partisan unit on this sabotage mission. Yidl in consultation with Eta had formulated the key strategy for this mission that the partisans were about to carry out.

Just a few miles from their encampment, a handful of the men laid out a few explosives along Road 63—a little south of Lukow. They would be near the road, ready to fire their guns quickly as the German trucks hit the explosives; a quick strike action that would hopefully yield little resistance. A little ways back from the main road was a second handful of the partisans, including Eta, who would come out shooting should the first line of attack face a gunfight.

In Eta's small group was Chaim Grinbaum. He was muttering that he hoped he would not need to use his rifle today. Eta tried to keep him calm by softly telling him to stay focused and ready.

Just before dark came a small convoy of German trucks proceeding southbound along Road 63, where Eta's partisan unit lay in wait. It was the size they were hoping to attack. They saw the trucks from a distance, heading their way. Staying absolutely quiet, they were now poised in crouched positions and gripping their weapons, ready to go into action. Then a large boom from an explosion sounded, followed by gunfire from the side of the road. Yidl and his group hit their target. The trucks were disabled and the few German forces inside were killed before they knew what hit them. Eta and her second line of defense group came running up, elated to see the quick strike work so effectively. Cheering could be heard among some in this small group of partisans. Chaim had a look of relief on his face.

The captured cargo of food and some weapons were quickly loaded into wagons the unit had on hand. The disabled trucks were then pushed off the road into ditches, and the bodies of the German soldiers tossed into the woods. The group acted quickly and then disappeared into the woods, with everyone having a bounce in their step. They had hit back against the Germans for the first time and succeeded beautifully in doing so. A good bounty with fortunately no casualties for the partisans. They were greeted with boisterous cheers when they returned to the camp with their captured loot.

Even Eta's father cracked a smile when the group of combatants returned with their loot and reported on their success. Tateh's ongoing state of depression would get worse when Eta would go away for a few days on her missions in the surrounding villages. When she returned to the partisan camp, Tateh would sometimes say to her that he was nothing but a burden. Eta would tell him to stop with such nonsense. His presence served as a strong motivation for her to return safely.

Fighting Back Against Collaborators

Around the same time (summer 1943) that Eta's partisan unit took their first action against the Germans, they also fought back against local Poles who harmed Jews and were collaborators with the Germans. Time to hit back.

One such known collaborator was the local chimney sweep in Lukow, a Mr. Jusicz. He celebrated when the Germans came in to occupy the town and continued to do so up through to the final liquidation of the ghetto. If he knew the whereabouts of any Jews attempting to hide, he happily shared the information with the Nazis. He knew all the Jewish homes in town and set out to discover their hiding places, taking for himself all the valuables that had been hidden away in each home—candlesticks, jewelry, clothing, cups, kitchenware, tablecloths, and much more. A special tablecloth of Eta's mother was among his vast stash of stolen property.

In the dark of the night, Eta and a small group of combatants from her partisan unit struck. They quietly slipped into town along back roads, with Eta leading them to the home of this evil chimney sweep. They broke into his house and forcefully woke up Jusicz and his wife. At gunpoint, they compelled him to take them to his shed where he stored much of the stolen valuables taken from his Jewish victims. Under pressure he confessed that he had more loot at a storage shed just down the road. They then took him to unveil all the items there. Between the two places, Eta's group ended up with two fully loaded wagons of all the stolen valuables, thanking the chimney sweep for providing one of the wagons.

Jusicz's house was somewhat on the edge of town. The partisans then took Jusicz into the fields in back of his home. A few quick shots later, the punishment was delivered. This evil man would never harm another Jew again. As Eta and her partisans worked their way back to the woods with all the valuables, they stopped at the home of one of their helpful farmers who had been a reliable food source for the unit. They gave him some of the items as a thank you for all of his help. He allowed them to store some of the items in the back of his barn. The rest of the bounty they took back to their camp and shared with partisan members. For instance, a recent addition to the partisan unit, a young man also from Lukow, Menachem Orlinsky, was provided with shoes he so desperately needed. The possessions Eta discovered from her own family—the tablecloth and shabbat candles, along with some of her own clothes—she kept for herself and shared with her father.

In another incident, Yidl was leading a scouting mission seeking food from farmers in the countryside, which the unit periodically did. David Rendel and Moshe Danyilak were part of this small group. In the distance they saw a small farmhouse. Sitting in the fields a few hundred yards or so away from this house was a young teenage boy. The boy had a crazed look in his eyes as they came upon him, a combination of fear and anger. Guessing the boy was Jewish, Yidl spoke Yiddish to help calm him down and assure him he was in no danger of harm from them. The men learned the boy was named Itche Meir and was 14 years old. Prior to the war, his parents had run a paint factory in Lukow.

A day or two before, per instructions from his parents, the boy had stayed back in the fields as his father and mother approached this farmhouse. They took the risk to approach this house and seek food from the farmer. When they knocked on the front door, the Polish farmer with his wife beside him opened up the door. Within a couple of minutes the conversation requesting food turned ugly. The farmer momentarily turned away from the front door and then quickly came back with a rifle and shot the boy's parents. Itche had witnessed the murder off in the distant fields. It was easy to understand why he had a crazed look in his eyes.

Yidl and his small group of partisans recommended something be done about this terrible betrayal and murder, and Itche heartily agreed. They quickly planned an attack on the farmhouse, intending to take the farmer and his wife by surprise. They then ran up to the farmhouse and Yidl banged on the front door a few times. The three men stood away from being seen and then barged in the slightly opened door with their guns pointed at the farmer and his wife nearby. Yidl then briefly explained to the Polish couple why they came calling, the transgressions they had carried out, with Itche glaring at them the whole time. No shots were fired. Instead, knifes were used to execute the farmer and his wife, with the boy making the final gash to cut off their heads. All the food they could find in the house was gathered and the group returned to their camp with this young teen, who never looked normal or happy again.

Eta and her partisan unit, now 80 or so strong, was standing up for itself while living in the woods. The reprisals the partisan group carried out against the local Poles in the villages and countryside, with more to come in time, created fear among many of the locals. These actions, as a result, led to the partisan members more openly receiving food when they came calling on some of these Polish villagers and farmers for help. Finding Jews who were in hiding throughout the countryside would soon take on an even greater importance as well.

9

$\mathcal{B}$uilding the Rescue Network

In 1943, as summer rolled into fall, and fall into winter, Eta and her partisan unit had a few more successful surprise attacks on German convoys coming through Road 63. A few of the men had gotten quite good at bomb making and demolition. Eta herself had proved to be a good shot when needed on these attacks. No one had been seriously hurt and the bounty gained each time was very helpful for the whole unit. Chaim Grinbaum still got away without firing his rifle.

Building Up—Supplies and Local Relations

With the bounty gathered from Jusicz, the chimney sweep from Lukow, along with some of the items gained from the attacks on the Germans, Eta was often able to barter with farmers and villagers to gain food for her whole partisan unit. Some of these local peasants appreciated the attacks carried out on the German occupiers, who took food and goods from them with no compensation, that they sometimes gladly supplied Eta's unit with food and supplies. No need to conduct any secret raids to steal food now.

Eta would also periodically sneak into Lukow and visit regularly with Dr. Kiernicki there. The good doctor would take time to continue his medical lessons with her, teaching her how to take out bullets, treat wounds, and set broken bones. He would then supply her with medicine to take back to her camp. As the months got cold, the unit had its well-built and snug underground bunkers that helped. As a result of the cooperation built with local farmers, sometimes small groups of eight to 10 people from her camp could find shelter with farmers' barns to gain warmth overnight.

As Eta continued carrying out her missions under the persona of the Christian woman Elizabeth, she would learn from some local Poles about Jews that had been seen hiding. On occasion, she would even come across a stray Jew in the woods as she was heading back to her partisan camp. In one such instance, she found a nine-year-old Jewish girl hiding in the woods with her mother. The girl broke a leg jumping off a deportation train on its way to a death camp. Eta picked up the injured girl and told her mother to follow her. She assured them that they were safe now. She brought them back to her partisan camp and mended the girl's leg. In a short while the young girl became a regular contributor in the unit, helping with activities in the camp, such as laundry and cooking.

Setting the Rescue Strategy and Striking Back Too

But how many more stray Jews in hiding the partisan unit could shelter and care for became a more regular topic of conversation between Eta, Yidl, and a few of the men. No one argued against the idea of wanting to save any Jew they could find. Eta was the most outspoken for doing this. But the concern the men had was how their camp could absorb more people—especially women, children, and the elderly. They were keeping up feeding the 80 or so Jews in their unit currently, but that was no simple task. Unless the stray Jews found were men with weapons or had special skills, such as a doctor or medic, it would be more difficult to absorb more than a few noncombatants into their unit in the woods. Eta understood the concern.

In Eta's discussion with Yidl and the others, they reasoned that if local farmers and villagers would be willing to shelter these Jews, it would create much less strain on the partisan unit. In their favor was that Eta's ongoing missions as Elizabeth Bryczemak, in the villages surrounding the forest, built good relations with some of the local Poles. So that became the strategy that Eta would take the lead in pursuing.

Still, Eta knew she had to be careful. For every helpful local Pole, there could be twice as many who would never help Jews, let alone some locals who were ready to betray them. In fact, not long before the last meeting on this topic of sheltering Jews that finalized the strategy to pursue, a local Pole around 60 years old had approached Eta as she was out on one of her missions. She had met the man previously and knew his son was involved in the AK in the vicinity. But this man had always been helpful towards her despite the fact that he suspected she was Jewish. It made no difference to him as he had told her when mentioning his suspicion in a past conversation. The local Polish man told her he had heard about a grave dug recently filled with Jews who had been caught and killed in a nearby village.

The next day Eta brought Yidl and a small group of combatants from her unit, including Chaim Grinbaum, David Rendel, and Moshe Danyilak to investigate. They found a shallow grave with a Jewish woman and her two small children buried in it.

The partisan unit waited until darkness and then approached the few homes of this little village in the vicinity of this makeshift grave. Yidl ordered the people in these homes to come out instantly or he and his unit would open fire. Everyone came out and in a short time confessed what involvement they had in the murder of these three Jews.

Eta suggested that their homes be set on fire to set an example for people to see what happens when they harm Jews. Soon thereafter the flames lit up the night sky, and howls could be heard from these villagers who lost their homes. As Eta saw it, justice had been served. These villagers were never to bother any Jews again.

In another instance of betrayal that winter of 1943-44, five members of Eta's partisan unit stayed at a farm house one night. As the group was ready to turn in for the evening, the farmer's son went out and reported them to the local authorities. During the night a German force came to the farmhouse. The partisans engaged the Germans in battle, killing some, but all the partisans died in the fight. Later on, members of Eta's unit came back to the farmer's house to exact revenge. They burned down the farmer's house and shot dead the son trying to escape, the one most responsible for the betrayal.

As 1943 rolled into 1944, Eta's partisan unit was gaining a reputation for hitting back against local Poles who collaborated with the Germans and local authorities who directly hurt Jews. But would there be enough courageous friends among the local Poles to help shelter Jews in need?

Gaining Traction with the Rescue Network

As Eta would regularly learn about the whereabouts of Jews here and there hiding in fields, woods, and the barns of local peasants, she would make contact with these Jews. Most were women and children. On their behalf, she took the risk of asking locals with whom she thought she had a good relationship if they would take in a person or two to care for and hide. Whether they knew Eta was Jewish or not was never discussed. Eta had a good sense of the people; she received mostly responses of yes to her requests for help. Stanislaw, her contact with the AL, at times also suggested helpful sources who would take in a person or two.

Finding these stray Jews and getting them into shelter with local Poles willing to be helpful became a vital part now of Eta's missions in the villages. "My job mostly was to save lives," was a reflection Eta would share years later in documentary videos about this risky rescue work.

The biggest help in this endeavor came from a woman referred to as Renata Marcinniak. The talk was that this woman was actually born in Lukow and raised there as Jewish, although Eta had not known her before. Prior to the war, she had left her husband and three children and had fallen in love with a Catholic Polish man. He had lived in a village a few miles away from Lukow, not far from Eta's partisan camp. She had converted to Catholicism. When her ex-husband was killed by the Nazis, Renata was able to get her three children out of the ghetto and hidden in the local village. Renata, likely in her mid-40s, had a very persuasive influence about her. Her current husband was supportive of her efforts too.

As Eta got to know Renata better, she started to bring to her the so-called stray Jews she found. Renata would then find local peasants to take in the Jews. It seemed whomever she asked in her village and beyond cooperated with her, allowing Eta to get these Jews placed into shelter. These Jewish refugees were often housed in the barns of these cooperative farmers and villagers, but they were now no longer living under these elements of the outdoors and wondering when they might next find food. The placement of these stray Jews increased. Eta reported progress to Yidl and the other men in her partisan unit. They remained on guard to strike back should any local Poles betray these Jews taken in or their Polish Catholic helpers.

As Eta continued carrying out her missions as Elizabeth to gather food, weapons, and intelligence for her partisan unit, checking in with Renata became a regular part of her route. With Renata trusting and confiding in her regarding recent activities, Eta would sometimes check in on the Jews hidden in local peasants' homes and bring food and supplies too, which was always much appreciated. With Renata, who seemed to know who among the locals could be trusted and helpful, as the point person of this rescue network, Eta felt confident that saving Jews beyond her partisan camp was working. As the winter months rolled into 1944, the number of Jews taken into the homes of the local villages had grown to an estimated 100 people.

Making a life in America now; Eta and Henry enjoy a New Year's eve celebration with the Lukower Society in New York City to bring in 1954.

Eta's service work in later yards brought her to Israel many times,
where she often met with distinguished Israeli leaders at ceremonies.
Here she is with Leah Rabin, wife of Prime Minister Yitzhak Rabin, 1970s.

Here at an AKIM event in Tel Aviv, Eta visits with renowned Holocaust
author, scholar, and Nobel Peace Prize winner Elie Wiesel.

Cousin Liza Melnick (like a fourth child to Eta) with Eta's son, Hal Wrobel, in front of memorial to Eta honoring her AKIM work in Herzilya, Israel, 2009.

Henry and Eta's three children—Anna Wrobel, Hal Wrobel, Shain Fishman—for a reunion in Portland, Maine, summer of 2016.

The next generation of family: Henry and Eta's eight grandchildren at a family Bar Mitzvah in Barnard, Vermont, August 2014. L to R: David Fishman, Sarah Fishman, Mara Gossack (Shain's children); Corinna Dodson (her son Elijah was having the Bar Mitzvah), Barak Wrobel (Anna's children); Leah Wrobel, Esther Wrobel, Tovah Wrobel (Hal's children).

Eta's gravestone where she is buried alongside Henry at the United Hebrew Cemetery in Staten Island, NY.

אשת חיל גיבורת
מלחמה ושלום
חיאטה בת פנחס חייט

ETA CHAIT

DEVOTED WIFE, MOTHER
GRANDMOTHER
HEROINE OF WAR AND PEACE

APRIL 2, 1916 – MAY 26, 2008

AND WE REMEMBER... זכור
PINCHAS AND SHAINDEL CHAIT

CHAIM SHULEM
MIRIAM SARA   FRAIDA
YAKOV MOISHE   FAIGA
CHANA   JOSHUA WOLF
MAIER JEHUDA   AZRIEL NOAH

10

Challenges and Close Calls

The routine of partisan life in the woods could sometimes be quiet and boring. Working to stay warm in the winter, finding and rationing food so everyone was fed and not starving, replenishing supplies, keeping the camp as clean as possible under the circumstances, and staying out of sight were regular aspects of this regimen. The occasional sabotage attack on a German convoy or the taking out of a local Pole for betraying Jews would spice things up, but so-called boring was actually good.

The alternative was far worse as everyone knew. One major incident alone—a raid by the Germans or a major attack by the AK or local Polish police on the hunt for Jews—would turn their world upside down instantly. So Eta, with Yidl's help, kept reminding people in their camp to be vigilant and to always keep their guard up. The ever-looming threat of danger never allowed one to be completely relaxed. Even when moments of levity came, such as when people sometimes rolled into one another in their sleep inside their tight bunkers, those moments were fleeting.

Needing to Stay on the Move

The hope of their partisan camp remaining secluded in the forest and undetected would not last. Possibly around early fall of 1943, Yidl awoke one morning and was walking in long johns towards a creek nearby. He was startled to see a middle-aged Polish man staring at him. Yidl grabbed a pitchfork he had close by and started screaming. The man started screaming with him and then ran away.

Before breakfast was over, Yidl with Eta and a few other men decided it was best to move the whole camp. Before nightfall they had moved everyone a little deeper into the woods and a little farther away from Lukow. Over the course of the next few days, they had built a new camp with its bunkers and cooking facilities.

Then a little bit later in the early winter months, a band of AK men attacked the outer edges of the unit's campsite. Their hand grenades blew up one of the bunkers where a handful of women and children usually slept. Seven people were killed in this surprise attack, including the only elderly person in the unit besides Eta's father. She was a grandmother whose daughter and five youths died with her in the attack—most of whom had been Jews Eta had found in the woods or villages and brought into the partisan camp for safety. The woman's grandson, age 17, had been working away from the camp with Eta and a few others at the time. He was devastated upon returning to the camp. Devastation and anger hit Eta. The partisan unit soon after moved its campsite again.

Not long after this incident, Eta was on a scouting mission with a few men from her unit when they were surprised by a band of AK fighters who opened fire on them from behind. Everyone in Eta's small group hit the ground. Eta was okay at the moment but she knew some of her partisans had been hit. Caught off guard, Eta and her group had not had a chance to defend themselves, and now this AK group was approaching them. A few of the Jewish men and Eta whispered among themselves to lie still and to play as if they were dead. This seemed like the best option under these very dangerous circumstances. Eta, lying on her back, stayed still with her gun nearby as she closed her eyes. Was this the end? She would not go down without taking a few of the vicious AK with her, she thought.

Fortunately, the shots fired from this AK band were heard at the main partisan camp, which was not that far away from where Eta and her scouting group had gone. A group of men from the main partisan camp then came running in their direction with rifles ready to fire, including Chaim Grinbaum. Seeing the larger numbers coming in their direction, the AK band ran away quickly. Eta was not hurt, but as the medic for the partisan unit, she soon would be tending to a couple of men who had been wounded. Two other men who had been with her would be buried. Soon after, the partisan group moved its campsite once again.

In another incident during the winter of 1943–44, Chaim Grinbaum and five other men from the partisan group were sleeping one night in the home of a local Polish woman who had been helpful. As mentioned previously, this was a practice the partisan members sometimes engaged in to help them get through the tough winter. In the middle of the night, Chaim woke up as he heard footsteps walking hurriedly towards the house. A hand grenade was thrown into the house. A band of AK fighters were upon them. Chaim scooped up the grenade and threw it outside. He, with partisan member Henoch Norman right behind him, ran out of the house and got away. The other four partisans who had been with them were killed. Now sleeping outside the partisan camp had grown quite risky.

Sometimes Eta would meet with Yidl and a few other men from the unit away from the camp in the homes and barns of friendly farmers on the outskirts of the woods. They would discuss strategy and plans during dinner. As 1944 rolled around, they had learned from some local Poles in the villages and farms who secretly listened to their radios—the Germans had outlawed radios and confiscated them where they could—that the Red Army was making advances against the German forces.

Two years before, the Soviet Union was near collapse from the German invasion. With the Soviet victory at Stalingrad in February 1943, the Red Army was slowly but steadily advancing forward throughout Eastern Europe, which before had been occupied by Nazi Germany. The latest broadcasts had the Soviet forces nearing the Bug River, not too far to the east of where Eta and her partisan unit were.

At the same time, the scuttlebutt that Eta had learned from the locals in her intelligence-gathering efforts was that the AK, the Polish Home Army, was very fearful of this potential communist incursion into Poland. They took the stance that all Jews were communists anyway and, therefore, had to be killed.

That evening at the farmhouse as Eta was having dinner with Yidl and David Rendel, a discussion of what to do with the ever-growing threat from the AK was top of the list of issues. As darkness drew down upon them, the partisan member Menachem Orlinsky, standing guard in front of the house, yelled to Eta and the two men inside that there was company in the fields. He suspected that at least a group of a half dozen men were sneaking up their way.

The AK was on the hunt again. Upon hearing the warning, Yidl grabbed his rifle and went out the front door. Eta and David followed right behind with their guns. At the top of his lungs, Yidl shouted, "Men take your positions! The AK is here on the attack," and then he fired a volley of shots in the direction of the fields.

Orlinsky also fired his rifle in the same direction. This gave the impression that a big group of partisans were at the farmhouse.

What was heard after this ploy were loud feet stomping through the snow and running away into the night as fast as they could. Everyone went back inside the house and waited for a short while. When all was quiet, Eta and the men went out into the fields where the AK group had been, saw footprints and gained a few rifles that had been left behind when the group had run off.

Carrying Out Justice Internally

Part of Eta's work during her missions into the villages and farms to gather food and weaponry was done through bartering. She would trade what valuables the unit had collected, such as jewelry and household items, to get the goods the partisans needed. After a few months, the shock lessened for 14-year-old Itche Meir, the boy taken into the partisan unit after his parents had been murdered by a local farmer. Slowly he began to talk a little more. One day he mentioned to Yidl and Eta that his parents had secretly hidden away gold they had. He knew that gold could greatly help the partisan unit in purchasing valuable supplies. Eta and Yidl were pleased to see how the boy wanted to contribute and help the cause.

Soon after at a gathering of the members of the partisan camp, Eta and Yidl spoke to the group and explained about Itche Meir's idea of finding the hidden gold, which according to Itche was likely in a cast-iron pot buried in the ground on the outskirts of Lukow. Then Eta said to the group, "We probably need just two or three men to go help Itche find his parents' hidden gold." Right away a big strapping man in the unit pulled a smaller man with him and stepped forward, saying, "We would be happy to carry out this mission with the boy." Everyone then nodded in agreement that having these two men assist Itche would be fine.

The two men who volunteered to go with Itche to find the gold were brothers-in-law. The one who was small in stature had been a shoemaker before the war. The big man used to work in a slaughterhouse.

So off they went the next morning on this mission with Itche to search for the hidden gold. A couple of days later the two men came back, but Itche was not with them. They told the story that the boy had changed his mind about revealing where the gold was and had run off on his own. Everyone shook their head in disappointment. But Eta and a few others were suspicious. Why would a 14-year-old boy who had been rescued by this partisan unit and offer to help the unit obtain gold suddenly change his mind and run away?

A few days later as Eta was out as Elizabeth selling her wares to some villagers, one of them, whom she had done business with before, told her he found a fresh grave not too far down the road from his home. Eta's suspicions started gnawing at her.

When Eta returned to her camp later that afternoon, she quietly asked David Rendel and Chaim Grinbaum to go with her to find this grave. The directions she got from the customer turned out to be accurate, as that evening Eta with David and Chaim found the fresh grave not far off the road. Digging it up, they found Itche's body with his head bashed. In her mind, Eta knew right away that this was not the work of local Polish collaborators.

When they returned to their camp, Eta had Yidl and Moshe Danyilak join her with David and Chaim to confront the two brothers-in-law. The two suspects were pulled aside. Eta spoke, revealing that they had found the murdered body of Itche Meir and then firmly and directly asked, "Why did you kill him?"

The smaller man, the former shoemaker, instantly broke. Amidst his tears, he confessed what had happened. His bulky brother-in-law had hit Itche on the head with his rifle butt. His hopes to steal the gold had been frustrated as Itche was having trouble remembering where it had been hidden. The shoemaker even wondered out loud, "I don't know why he allowed me to live since I witnessed his savage attack on the boy. I wish I could have protected the boy." The shoemaker felt extremely guilty about what had happened. Then Eta and her small group turned to the large man and sternly asked, "What do you have to say about this?" The man said nothing and just stared into the distance, while holding tightly to his rifle. They let the situation be for the moment.

A short time later Eta said to her small group of allies, "We need to take this big man's weapon away from him before anything else happens." That night while the big man slept, Eta with her four confidants, snuck up and quietly took away his rifle. They then met privately and discussed the next steps to take. The decision was made to let the small brother-in-law live due to his confession. They didn't want to lose any more Jews from their partisan unit. On the other hand, they decided they could not trust the big brother-in-law. There was no way they could have a murderer of Jews in their camp. They were all in agreement; no debate was necessary.

The next morning, a few men from the partisan unit, with rifles drawn, were assigned to escort the big man deep into the woods. Once there, they executed him. No one felt good about what was done, but Eta and the others recognized this justice in the woods had to be carried out for the safety and greater good of the partisan group.

Encountering Dangers On Her Elizabeth Missions

As Eta carried out her missions to the farms and villages outside her unit's camp in the woods, to the outside world she was Elizabeth Brycemak—a Polish Catholic woman with her long brown hair in braids, visibly wearing a cross. When she returned to the camp, sometimes having been gone two to three days at a time, she would be told that her father had been quietly sobbing while she was gone.

Tateh, in his ongoing state of depression, would worry even more when Eta was away from the partisan camp. He knew, as Eta knew herself, that these missions or excursions carried high risk and danger. Plus, Eta usually went unarmed so as to not create suspicion as to why a woman would carry a gun.

Sure enough, close calls occurred periodically that nearly led to Eta's capture and likely execution. For instance, one day early on as she started her missions as Elizabeth, Eta was walking on a road on the outskirts of Lukow. Looking on from a distance was a Polish boy who recognized her from when she worked at Mr. Dietz's chicken factory. He started shouting that a Jew is coming and someone should call the Gestapo to get her. A man nearby came over to the boy and grabbed him by the neck, telling him to stop his screaming. The man then yelled in Eta's direction to get away. Eta then took off running in the opposite direction down the road, but she did not run into the woods right away so as to avoid the impression that the forest was where she came from. After a few minutes and now out of sight and out of shouting distance, she then darted back into the woods and away from Lukow. She had narrowly escaped with the unexpected help of this unknown man.

A few months later this same man one day had wandered into the woods and stumbled upon a corner of Eta's partisan camp. Men from the camp had captured him. Usually letting any local Pole go free and stay alive was a move the partisan members viewed as too risky to make. They knew that it only took one person to betray the group to the local authorities or the Nazis. When Eta came over to investigate the commotion, she instantly recognized the man as the one who had saved her from the screaming boy near Lukow. He was on his knees, pleading for his life and saying he would never tell anyone, including his wife, about this camp of Jews in the woods. Eta intervened and told everyone how helpful this man had been to her and how he had likely saved her life. She ordered the partisans to let him go. He ran off quickly and never betrayed them, as she trusted he would not do so.

Later on, another instance of unexpected help would save Eta, as Elizabeth, from certain harm. As excursions continued, Eta began to develop good relationships with local Polish farmers and villagers with whom she would see periodically to do business or to tutor their children. She simply became known as the young woman from Warsaw who often had something to sell and always came with a friendly and polite manner. In this particular instance, it was a Sunday afternoon and Eta was about to call upon a farmer and his wife whom she had seen the day before. She had indicated to them that she might be back the next day to do more business.

She had never asked this couple if they knew of any stray Jews that might be hiding in the vicinity. She kept her conversations to business or the latest hardships of life under German rule. On this Sunday afternoon, as she was walking in the fields toward this farmhouse, the farmer's wife came running out and intercepted her. She told Eta not to continue onto the house. Inside was a group of AK men having a party with some women and her son. They were dancing and drinking. Eta could hear music coming from the house in the distance. The farmer's wife then startled Eta by telling her that she knew Eta was a Jew and had known it all along. She recognized that if Eta came to the house it would mean trouble for her and warned her to stay away for today. While Eta did not know how this woman knew she was a Jew, she thanked the farmer's wife for the warning and proceeded in the opposite direction.

Saved again by another courageous and caring Pole giving Eta a little unexpected help.

Sometimes through premonition and a constant internal self-talk with her grandmother and mother, Eta was helped in escaping from danger. She often thought she could hear their voices in her mind speaking to her. And she was determined to listen when these voices spoke to her.

One evening Eta was departing Lukow to return to her camp in the woods. She had gone to see Dr. Kiernicki and his wife Maria in Lukow to receive more training on surgical techniques for treating wounds and to be given medical supplies to take back. As she departed, nightfall had set in. Heading down the road leading out of town, she saw in the distance a few people sitting in the ditches smoking cigarettes. The internal voices told her not to go any further in that direction.

Eta stopped at the first farmhouse she came upon a few minutes later, which was not a place she had called on before. Lights were still on in the house, so she knocked. Opening the door was a large man. Behind him Eta could see a woman sitting meekly in the corner of the room. Eta, in her perfect Polish, explained that she was on her way to see her aunt in the next village but had lost track of time and did not want to be out on the roads past curfew and risk being arrested. She asked if she could sleep in the front room of the man's home until daybreak. The big man said that was where his sister slept, but that Eta could join him in the big room down the hall that had a large bed in it. It was where he slept but there was room for both of them. Eta politely declined. Then the farmer told her that she could sleep in his barn, and he directed her towards it.

After he went back in the house, the internal voices in Eta told her not to stay there. So instead, she went into the bushes away from the house rather than going inside the barn. Sure enough, a few minutes later she could hear the man rumbling through the barn looking for her and cursing as he did, wondering where she went. She was thankful those voices spoke to her and that also this man did not suspect that she was Jewish. She made it back to camp the next morning.

If Eta needed a safehouse in the vicinity for a night, she could sleep at the farm and home of the Glawinski couple. Jan and Maria would welcome her when she came by, feeding her and allowing her to stay the night if she needed. While the Germans seldom went into the woods in Eta's area to track down her partisans, they did come into the villages periodically, usually to collect food.

As Eta was working her way back to her camp one afternoon, she stopped by to pay a visit to Jan and Maria. After being in the house for a short while, Jan spotted out of the corner of the front window a group of Germans coming down the road on foot. He saw uniforms and glanced away quickly, not knowing whether the approaching group coming was full of soldiers or Gestapo. Either way, a major problem faced all of them. Jan spoke quickly in a stressed-out voice for Eta to run out the back door. Maria, handling the situation more calmly, knew that taking that move to avoid capture was too risky. So she quickly led Eta to a ladder and had her climb up into their attic to hide. Maria then moved the ladder away from the attic so as not to arouse suspicion. As Eta climbed into the attic. She moved herself into a position that enabled her to lie down quietly on the straw that helped insulate the attic.

The Germans shortly thereafter banged on the front door and entered the home of the Glawinski couple. But this seemingly perfect hiding place proved to be not so perfect after all. The attic was full of mice. As Eta attempted to lie still and be quiet, mice started crawling all over her and even up the legs of her pants. She did all that she could not to squirm and scream, praying again to her grandmother and mother as well as to God to save her. She could hear voices and barking dogs downstairs. An excruciating half hour passed before the noise downstairs cleared. No harm had been done to the Glawinski couple. Jan brought the ladder out and climbed up the attic to tell Eta that it was safe to come down now. Eta was frozen. Jan called Maria to come help. They jumped into the attic and warded off all the mice, helping Eta then crawl back down. It took Eta a good three hours before she was over the horror of the ordeal. But again her prayers were answered, and she had escaped certain danger.

When Eta finally made it back to her partisan camp, her medic skills were called upon right away. This helped her put the ordeal at the Glawinski home behind her. The partisan member Henoch Norman, sometimes called Noach, had gotten ill. Eta knew what medicines with which to treat him, and he recovered soon after to full strength. Noach somehow mistook Eta's medical care as her way of showing him love, which he fondly appreciated. After this treatment, he would sometimes hover around Eta when she was in the camp, desiring to be near his love. For Eta, there was no love interest at all. For her instead, Noach was a real pest—a nuisance amidst the dangers of partisan life in the woods.

***D*evastation to Liberation**

March 1944. Eta had now been a partisan in the woods for nearly a year. Overall, she and her partisan unit were functioning well.

Feeling a Sense of Hope

Temperatures were now above the freezing mark. There was a sense of hope that spring would not be too far off. The winter of 1943-44 had not impeded the partisan unit. They had been able to keep everyone fed. Plus, with the help of some local farmers, they could get shelter at night quite often. Usually in small groups of eight to ten, the partisans would sleep in the barns of these farmers, lessening the effect of the cold and snow of the winter.

The partisan group had now lost about one-fourth of its members from its peak of eighty in the past summer. The AK, much more so than the Germans, was the main culprit for these casualties. Surprise attacks, as mentioned previously, and occasional direct combat skirmishes with AK bands started to become part of life in the woods. But Eta and her all-Jewish partisan unit had fought off these attacks and usually inflicted more casualties on the AK than suffering themselves, so there was still a sense of hope that the group was holding its own as well as could be expected. Interestingly enough, Chaim Grinbaum had still not fired his rifle. He had either been away on food missions when these clashes happened or had run away fast enough when the surprise attack occurred on the farmhouse in which he had been sleeping.

In addition, the partisan unit had carried out a few more sabotage attacks on German convoys, blowing them up on the main road from Lukow to Radzyn. Despite the attacks, the Germans had not come into the woods to hunt down the Jewish partisan unit. Because these raids were quick and decisive, the thinking of Eta's group was that the Germans were not sure who had hit them and likely thought the AK was responsible.

As a result, confidence was building among Eta's partisan unit that they could ably defend themselves and that they could go after local Poles who harmed any Jews they had placed into hiding. On her missions into the villages, Eta often stopped by to see her primary helper, Renata Marcinniak, and the Jews who had been given shelter in to the homes of local Poles. There were now approximately one-hundred such stray Jews who had found shelter and were holding up well under the challenging circumstances. This was another cause for hope in March of 1944. In addition, with the news Eta had gathered in her missions about the advances of the Soviet Red Army against the Germans to the east, there was hope in many people's minds within the partisan unit that the Soviet forces would soon drive the Germans out of the area.

Turning from Hope to Devastation

As March 1944 came, the partisan unit had relocated its camp back to its original place in the woods not far from Lukow. Eta, Yidl, David, Chaim, and Moshe, along with a few others, strategized that being close to Lukow again might be in the best interest of their group. They calculated that when the Soviet forces advanced and drove the Germans out of this area of Poland, they would likely come through Lukow on their way to other major posts the Germans were holding.

The trek back to the original camp had required Eta to pull her father along most of the way, sometimes with the help of others. Tateh was now 58-years-old, but very frail. He could not walk much on his own. The loss of his spirit had greatly weakened his physical condition. As his health had been failing, his eyes were not very good either. He was in a constant state of depression, greatly agonizing over the loss of his family and especially his beloved wife, Mammushe, Eta's mother. Along the journey back to the original camp, he would sometimes tell Eta, "I should be left behind for the Germans or AK to get. That would be best for you and everyone else in the partisan group." Eta adamantly refused to let her father be left behind, directly telling him, "Stop that nonsense. I am not going to leave you anywhere. You stick with me and we will be fine."

Even before, when Eta would go away on her missions into the villages, she would find out from others in the partisan camp upon returning that her father had been crying most of the time. When she was in the camp, she would spend as much time as possible with her father. He would again say to her that he was too much of a burden, that she would be better off without him. She would have none of that and would tell him, "Tateh, you are very important in my life. Don't forget that. We have each other and never should we allow that to change."

Then one day in late March of 1944, Eta had been away overnight on one of her missions. When she returned to the partisan camp the next day, Tateh was nowhere to be found. No one knew where he was or when he might have slipped away. Eta frantically went running to find him. She first went to see a few farmers she knew who lived on the outskirts of Lukow to find out if they knew anything of her father's whereabouts. They reported that they had heard news of an old Jewish man who had wandered into the main street of Lukow and sat down there. The Gestapo had come upon on him and soon shot him dead on the spot.

Eta's heart was racing a mile a minute. She continued running right into Lukow. She went to the tearoom in the town center. She knew the Polish family who ran it, the Bielski family. They were friends of her father and family prior to the war. When she came in, Mr. Bielski recognized her right away. One part of him was smiling, elated as well as surprised to see Eta. On the other hand, he looked around warily to see if anyone else noticed she had come in. He took her to a back room to speak with her privately. Eta then blurted out what she had heard from the farmers and added, "Certainly these rumors must not be true."

Mr. Bielski then said, "Eta, what you heard from the farmers about your father at the hands of the Germans, I am so sorry to say is true. Indeed, the old Jewish man shot dead by the Gestapo was your father. They took his body and dumped it into a pile of dead Jewish bodies in the place that had once been the Jewish cemetery in town. Again, I am so sorry."

Eta was speechless. She could hardly breathe. Shock and pain ran through her mind and body. Mr. Bielski gave her something to drink, but she refused to eat anything when he offered her some food. She had to go.

Her face revealed the devastation of her loss. Even when he offered to give her some food to take along, she refused. The only items she took from him were cigarettes. He had his sons escort her back out of town and into the woods.

Eta was feeling too disoriented to make her way back to the partisan camp. She knew Jan and Maria's house was not too far away, so she went there. When she knocked on their door and Jan opened it up, she could not speak to him. He saw the grim look on her face, sensing she had just experienced a terrible loss, likely her father. He said something about this softly to Maria and had Eta sit inside the house for a short bit with his wife.

Jan then went out into the fields and quickly dug a bunker in the ground. He came back into the house and by hand guided Eta to this bunker. He placed her into it and covered it up with straw and wooden planks. It was enough space for Eta to lie in and that was all she did. This bunker was considered the safest place for her to stay in for an indefinite period of time.

Jan would literally crawl out at night from his house to the hole Eta was in to provide her food, so no one from the road could see him. But Eta refused to eat. All she did was lie in the tight bunker and occasionally smoke the cigarettes she had with her. Jan and Maria were very worried as were the people back in the partisan camp, wondering what had happened to Eta. Was she captured or worse, killed?

After Eta had been missing for a week, Yidl, Chaim, David, and Moshe went out on a scouting mission to see if they could find her. They too had heard the news about Eta's father. They started by calling upon the house of Jan and Maria Glawinski, who took them out to the bunker hole where Eta was lying. They then pulled her out of the hole and took her back to the camp.

But Eta was in a catatonic state. Her grief from the loss of her father was all-consuming. After a few days of Eta resting in the camp but still hardly eating anything, Yidl and the others were very worried. They did not want to see one of their beloved comrades and leaders die.

There was a woman that Eta had known, even before the war, who lived in a farm on the outskirts of Lukow. Referred to as Ludmila Radakourczyk, she was a widow with a couple of daughters who lived with her. Eta would sometimes stop at Ludmila's house on the way back from her missions to clean up and get something to eat. So the worried partisan men who had found Eta at the home of the Glawinski couple took Eta to the home of Ludmila, hoping she could help.

Ludmila took Eta in and immediately began to care for her. Eta was very filthy, as she had made no effort to clean herself in the past two weeks. Lice were in her hair as well. So Ludmila bathed Eta each day. She gave her some soup to eat and would talk to her softly, telling her that her life would go on and that she would be strong again. Eta could not sleep much. Images of her father kept racing through her mind. She could hear his voice talking to her. "Eta, you would be better without me. I am now an old man, a burden to you."

"No!" she would be yelling back in her mind. "You are not a burden. You are my father, my only family who is so dear to me. Please stop with this silly talk." Sadly, in his desire not to be a burden to his daughter, Tateh's giving up on his life had almost caused Eta to give up on hers.

After two weeks under Ludmila's care, Eta started showing signs of life again. Yidl, Chaim, David, and Moshe came to get her and bring her back to camp. They thanked Ludmila for all her help. Eta could walk on her own but would hold on to the back of Yidl's belt as she moved, something she would periodically continue to do over the next couple of months. Everyone was excited to see Eta when she returned to the camp. She had been gone for almost a month, as it was now late April 1944.

Fighting Towards Liberation

Eta continued to heal physically and emotionally, at least enough to be back in action helping to lead the partisan unit. Her return had raised everyone's spirits. But quiet time would now be hard to come by. Intelligence gathered from local Poles and from Stanislaw, Eta's contact with the AL, indicated that the Red Army was advancing across the Bug River deeper into Poland. As this happened, the AK in the area, now very worried about a communist takeover, mobilized and had put out the word that it was time to hunt down and kill the Jews.

In early May of 1944, a clash ensued between an AK band of fighters and Eta and her Jewish fighters. As the AK was in retreat, Eta got shot during the ongoing skirmish. She initially felt a sharp pain, something burning in her leg, but kept firing her gun until the battle was won. Sure enough, as she checked afterwards at the camp, she had been wounded in the leg. The bullet had lodged between her boot and the calf of her right leg, causing her leg to swell. As the unit's medic, she had helped take out bullets from her fellow partisans when they had been wounded. Now she was the wounded one, but her swollen leg made it impossible for her to pull her boot off to tend to her own wound. On the other hand, the pressure and tightness created by her boot kept her from bleeding out. So Eta kept moving, with a bullet stuck somewhere in her calf. Helping to keep this partisan unit going was too important for her to let this wound slow her down. Now, when she held on to Yidl's belt in the back, she did so for balance as much as for emotional support.

Over the next two months, periodic clashes with the AK continued. Eta and her group fought hard, but casualties started to mount. Eta spent a lot of her time tending to the wounded. Little thought was given to her own wounded leg. She kept working, moving, and fighting.

By the latter part of July 1944, fierce fighting erupted in and around Lukow. The Red Army had reached Lukow after coming across the Bug River in mid-July. The retreating Germans took a stand there. The town was getting bombed by both Soviet and German planes. Eta and her partisan unit kept its distance. The

AK was now nowhere to be found. After a week the fighting ended. The Germans were defeated. Their soldiers were killed, captured, or fled farther towards Warsaw. The Red Army took over Lukow.

The sudden air of silence was now filled with a downpour of rain. Because of her language skills, which included some broken Russian, Eta decided that she would venture out from the partisan camp into Lukow to assess the situation. Everyone stayed back to see what she would find out. Once again, the courage she showed was greatly admired by the others. Eta boldly marched with her slight limp towards town as the rain continued to come down. As she got closer to the edges of Lukow, she saw two soldiers ahead. She could tell by their uniforms that they were not Germans. She was both relieved and elated.

She went right up to the two soldiers and, in her coarse Russian, told them that she was a Jewish partisan from the woods nearby. One of the soldiers then grabbed Eta and started dancing with her in the rain, smiling and laughing as he did so. He was a Russian Jew. He asked Eta to take him and his fellow Red Army soldier to her partisan camp.

A little later, with the rain now stopped, Eta walked into the camp with the two soldiers. When she announced who these two soldiers were, that one of them was Jewish, and that the Germans had been defeated, everyone cheered and some even cried. Thirty-two members from her partisan unit were left in the group. The fighting against the AK over the last few months had taken a toll. Moshe Danyilak, David Rendel, Chaim Grinbaum, and Yidl Woland were part of this remaining thirty-two. Among the others in the all-Jewish partisan unit who were also there at the time of liberation and whose names were known were the young men: Menachem Orlinsky, Moishe Greizer, Nathan Herschberg, and Henoch Norman and a young woman named Fraida Fluk. The two soldiers then escorted everyone from the camp back to a place just outside Lukow. The Red Army had set up a base there, including a mobile hospital. Everyone was tended to and fed a warm and hearty meal.

Menachem Orlinsky, Moshe Greizer, and Fraida Fluk, now excited over being liberated, decided to go into Lukow. Unbeknownst to them, conditions were not safe as the town had been heavily mined by the Germans. When they saw a Red Army soldier on horseback ride nearby and get blown up by a mine, they quickly left Lukow and headed back to the military camp.

The next morning, Eta went into surgery for her wounded leg. She was in there for a few hours. The effort to cut off her boot to get at the wound took longer than the actual surgery to remove the bullet. No anesthesia was used. Eta was well used to the pain in her leg by now. A short time after being bandaged up tightly, she was up and walking—as good as new.

She subsequently went to work for the Soviet commander, using her German language skills to help interrogate hundreds of German troops who were now prisoners of war. The Red Army was working on clearing the mines in Lukow, making the town off limits.

So the next day, Eta and her whole partisan unit were transported by truck south to the Parczew Forest near Lublin where they hooked up with other Jewish partisans there. Among these partisans was the leader Chiel Grynzspan and a top lieutenant in his unit named Sam Gruber. Of the all-Jewish partisan units that operated within what would be Poland proper today, Grynzspan had the largest force. With him was a group of nearly 400 combatants, along with another roughly 400 noncombatants. He was in his mid-20s, not tall, but with broad shoulders. Grynzspan had a calm and easygoing demeanor about him. Eta was happy to visit with him and be among all these other Jews. By the end of July 1944, after 15 months in the forest, liberation had finally come for Eta Chait.

12

$\mathcal{L}$ife After Liberation

E ta now waited in the camp set up by the Red Army in the south near Lublin. She was anxious to return to Lukow, but the Soviet army was keeping people away until the German mines had been fully cleared. At the same time, a feeling of safety came to Eta. For the first time in not just the 15 months in the woods, but in the nearly five years since German forces invaded Poland, the daily Nazi terrorist threat was no longer hanging over her head.

However, German forces still remained in parts of Poland. The war was not done yet. On August 1, 1944, the Warsaw Uprising erupted. The Polish government-in-exile in London hoped that the Allies, especially the United States and Great Britain, would help it in setting up the new government in Poland after the war—one that would not be communist. With its Polish Home Army or AK resistance forces on the ground, the thinking of the Polish government leaders in London was that the best way to achieve this goal was to take the fight to the Germans. They would first drive them out of the major city of Warsaw and then finally expel them from the rest of Poland once and for all.

The Red Army was positioned just outside of Warsaw, yet stood idly by as the uprising ensued. The common thinking was the Soviet forces had been ordered by dictator Joseph Stalin to stand back, that this was his chance to greatly weaken the AK and reduce any eventual interference with his plans to create a postwar communist state out of Poland. Stalin would be proven right. After 63 days, the Warsaw Uprising was put down, and the AK was soundly defeated by the Germans.

Becoming Mayor of Lukow

In July 1944, around the same time the Red Army was driving German forces out of Lukow, back in Moscow the PKWN was established. Translated in English to mean the Polish Committee of National Liberation, the PKWN was Stalin's mechanism for reconstructing Poland as a communist country, which the Soviet Union could greatly influence and control after the war. Stalin paid no heed to the Polish government-in-exile.

As the Red Army started seizing areas in Poland, driving away the German occupation, provisional governments in these locales were being set up. PKWN members from the Soviet Union had come into Poland and were working with Poles, mainly those who had been part of the leftist, communist-sympathizing People's Army or the AL, to set up and run these provisional governments. The Polish Communist Party was now getting revitalized.

Eta was able to return to Lukow in the latter part of September 1944. She took up residence in an empty house in the middle of the town. The house had a bakery downstairs and many vacant rooms upstairs. Her hope was to find surviving members of her own family and take them to live in this house with her. No one came.

Eta then started going to the train station in Lukow and welcoming some of the displaced Jews who were coming back into town. Soon her once vacant house was filled with these surviving and returning Jews.

A short time later, a meeting was called in the town's marketplace led by a man from the AL. The marketplace in days of peace had been a great place for commerce and the gathering of the Jews and Catholics of Lukow. During the German occupation, it was turned into the roundup zone for gathering and deporting Jews to the Treblinka death camp. Now, scarred by war, a rally was taking place in this center of Lukow. Many youth from Lukow, a few surviving Jews and several non-Jews alike, were listening to this AL leader and Polish communist standing on a chair and talking about the importance of setting up a government to get Lukow running well again. People cheered, including Eta.

When the AL spokesman asked if anyone present could use a typewriter to help him keep records, Eta volunteered, "I can help." She was put to work right away.

The first main order of business was to see who wanted to be part of the local police department. Sixty young men volunteered, and Eta typed their names on this official government record. The AL rally leader announced that anyone who had collaborated with the Nazis and anyone who was still a member of the AK would not be allowed to have any positions in the new government. A decree by the PKWN in late August 1944 had made all secret military organizations now illegal and ordered them to be dissolved. This meant the AK, the Polish Home Army, was now not a legal entity and was officially out of business.

The next order of business the speaker declared was to select someone to be the mayor, which is an equivalent role to town administrator. Many in the gathering knew Eta from before the war and had seen how active she had been in helping since the liberation. They spoke up on her behalf, recommending her because of her good qualities and leadership skills. When the AL speaker turned to Eta and asked if she would like the job, she nodded her head affirmatively and said, "Yes, I can do this job and am glad to be of help at this time of need." Thus, Eta was now "elected" mayor of Lukow. Another man, believed to be an AL partisan fighter named Mr. Zdybski, was picked to be the secretary of the Polish workers, a common communist party role. He would work closely with her in running this new town government.

The business of setting up a government administration and getting all its services functioning kept Eta on the go. This was a good thing as it kept her mind away from constantly dwelling on the loss of her family. She was meeting newly-formed government representatives from Lukow's surrounding villages, coordinating services to discuss ways to adjust to this new life as part of the Polish Workers' Party—the communist party structure the Soviets liked to use. She was involved in helping ensure food was on hand for residents, schools got set up, health care was provided, and streets and sanitation services functioned.

Individuals would sometimes come to her office (now situated in a large building in town), and Eta would attempt to help however she could. For example, a large farm outside of town that the Germans had controlled was now vacated. She arranged for her dear helpers Jan and Maria Glawinski to obtain this farm and house—a much bigger and better place for them and their family to live.

Sometimes she served as a source of comfort. For instance, she met a young Jewish man who came to her office one day named Yankel Kesselbrenner. He originally was from Lukow and had survived in the woods in a different partisan group than Eta's. He was able to get his mother and two sisters hidden with a farmer, only to witness—from a distance—them being captured and murdered by an AK band of fighters just a few months before the area was liberated. Yankel was the youngest of seven children, and he now had only one sister left who had made it to Palestine before the war started. Within a couple of years, he would join his sister there. Yankel was a few years younger than Eta, and she had not known him before the war. But his loss and survival story, along with being a fellow Lukow inhabitant, created a bond between them. She would see him in the future.

Eta's role as mayor also involved assisting in security matters. She gladly let the Red Army officers know who the collaborators with the Nazis were as well as where AK members might be hiding. Warnings came to her of possible AK members infiltrating the ranks of the new Lukow police force. Along with Mr. Zydbski, they ordered an investigation that found a plot was brewing by former AK members to eliminate the new government in Lukow and that one of the plotters held a high-ranking position within the Lukow police. When the results of the investigation were handed over to the Soviet authorities, the police infiltrator shot himself dead. More than 200 men with ties to the AK who came marching into Lukow intent on rebellion were met by Red Army forces. They got rounded up and taken away, never to be seen again.

Along Comes Heniek Wrobel

As the fall of 1944 rolled on, Eta started getting visits to her office by a man named Heniek Wrobel, visits that were more social than business in nature. She had briefly met Heniek back in September not long after she had returned to live in Lukow. He was a Polish Jew serving in the Red Army who had come into Lukow at that time wondering if he had any family there. He then had returned to his army unit stationed outside Warsaw.

Although she had not met Heniek previously, she knew of him. Heniek grew up on the outskirts of Lukow. In their rural area, they were the only Jewish family. His older brother Avram had been friends with Eta's older brother Schulem. They were also distant cousins. Heniek's great aunt had married one of

Eta's uncles on her mother's side. Heniek was a couple of years younger than Eta. Unlike Eta, he had little formal education. He stood around five feet-seven inches and weighed around 145 pounds but was strong and athletic. He was known to climb trees in 60 seconds. He was also known to be socially active and outgoing. As a teenager prior to the war, he often came into Lukow to find a good time.

In September 1939, when Nazi Germany invaded and conquered Poland, Heniek, along with two of his brothers and one of his sisters, was able to leave the area of Lukow quickly and get across the Bug River into the Soviet eastern zone. They were later moved deeper into the Soviet Union and all survived because of it. A younger sister Sarah was able to survive in Warsaw under a false Catholic identity. Four other siblings and Heniek's parents did not survive the Holocaust.

In 1941, after a year working on a collective farm in Russia, Heniek was drafted into the Red Army. Sometime in late summer of 1944, as the Red Army was making its push into Poland to drive the German forces out, Heniek was severely wounded in battle. A bullet wound to his head had put him into a coma for three weeks; doctors thought he was dead. When he started to move his pinky finger, doctors rushed him into surgery and brought him back to life.

In early fall of 1944, around two months after he and Eta had met briefly, Heniek got leave from his army unit to recover from his serious injury. He had returned to Lukow and came calling on Eta Chait. Eta, now age 28, was a very independent woman— like a woman from years ahead of her time, not from the era of the 1940s. Getting into a committed relationship and then marriage was not on her mind or of great interest to her at this time. She had already rebuked the advances of Henoch (Noach) Norman, the partisan from her unit whom she had tended to in her role as the group's medic when he was ill while living in the woods. His gratitude for this care turned him into a nuisance to Eta; he constantly expressed his interest in her whenever he saw her.

When he came back to Lukow and she was now mayor, she bluntly told Noach to find someone else for his affections and to stay away from her. In addition, she was regularly getting marriage proposals from Russian Jews serving in the Red Army, which she politely turned down. Soon, though, Eta found herself going out after work with Heniek nearly every day. She had a favorable impression of him and enjoyed spending time with Heniek. He was looking for a serious relationship, but she was still uncertain.

She even left town overnight, calling it government business and not telling Heniek she was going to be away. Her uncertainty about getting serious caused her to want to create distance. But Heniek was persistent and tracked her down. That move impressed Eta and made her happy.

A short time later back in Lukow, as Eta walked into her office that morning, there was Heniek sitting in his usual chair that he hung out in when he visited her. Before she could settle in for the work of her day, Heniek, without hesitation, spoke up, "Eta, I know what we need in our lives at this time. Would you marry me?"

Eta's gut reaction to the marriage proposal took over. She initially exclaimed a strong "No!" to the proposal. Heniek shot back. "If you stick to this position, no need for me to stick around here. I would leave you and not return."

Eta took a breath. This courtship had been a mere six weeks, but she realized that the time had come to get on with life and that meant living with someone who loved you rather than being alone. She then smiled and said, "Yes, Heniek. I accept your proposal for marriage." He jumped in joy, and they warmly embraced and kissed each other.

On December 20, 1944, in one of the Soviet offices in Lukow with some Russian Jewish soldiers on hand to informally officiate, Eta and Heniek got married. The ring Heniek put on her finger was borrowed and was given back to its owner soon after.

Moving On From Poland

As 1945 rolled around, the Soviet forces continued their advances in Poland, driving German forces back into Germany. On January 17, 1945, the country's capital and largest city Warsaw, or what was left of it, was liberated by the Red Army. The next day the liberation of Krakow, which had been home to the Nazis' capital and government base in conquered Poland, was also completed. The brutal Nazi ruling governor of Poland, Hans Frank, fled back to Germany just in time to escape capture.

On January 27, 1945 the Auschwitz-Birkenau death camp, the remnants of who and what was left, was liberated by the Red Army. That date today serves as the United Nations International Holocaust Remembrance Day. The rest of the fighting in World War II was now taking place in Germany. The Red Army from the east and Allied forces of Great Britain, Canada, the United States, and other countries from the west were closing in. Germany officially surrendered on May 7, 1945.

In the meantime, the city of Lodz, some 160 miles due west of Lukow, was liberated by the Red Army at the same time as Warsaw. Soon after the liberation of the city, Eta's communist bosses ordered her to go to Lodz to help in the forming of the new government there. Eta had lived and worked in Lodz as did her family for a period in the 1930s up until the start of the war, so she was looking forward to returning to this city where her early years of adulthood began. She and Heniek got to stay in a very nice house that had been vacated by the Germans.

While on assignment in Lodz, Eta realized she was now pregnant. Not only was this occurring early in her marriage with Heniek, but the pregnancy was not expected at all. Eta had wondered after the last few years of irregular periods in the trying times she lived through if she could even get pregnant.

RSecond thoughts hit Eta regarding her relationship with Heniek. She remembered Heniek's words through their fast courtship into marriage. He had talked about how it was time for them to have fun in their lives for a while, after having that experience taken away over the last number of years. So when Eta informed Henry she was pregnant, she told him, "You are not obligated to continue in this marriage and you're free to be released from it. I would understand if you wanted to move on elsewhere in your life. I know this was not something planned or expected. It's okay to go have fun in your life at this time."

Heniek Wrobel was having none of it. Without hesitation, he let Eta know, "Look, if parenthood is hitting us sooner than expected, then so be it. I am ready to move forward and have a long life with you and our new family. I have no regrets." Eta's doubts of his love or commitment did not surface again.

Within a month or so of working in Lodz, Eta was then transferred to help communist government-forming efforts in Breslau, Germany (today part of Poland). She and Heniek moved again. Heniek even started running a restaurant while in Breslau. While there, on September 25, 1945, their first child Hershel Pinchas was born. He was named after both of their fathers.

Approximately five weeks after their son was born, Eta had visitors come one day to her office in Breslau. The visitors were two Soviet communist party operatives. They came to give her "good news." She, with arrangements made for her family to join her, would be going to Moscow for a month of training that would help her in running the new Poland. They were all to leave the next day.

That night Eta broke the news to Heniek. There was no way she wanted to become a professional communist let alone contend with what might happen if the party bosses back in the Soviet Union found out she was a Jew. Heniek wholeheartedly agreed. He went to work right away, arranging for their get-away.

That night, or rather in the wee hours of the next morning, the Wrobel family caught a train out of Breslau to Berlin. Heniek's younger sister Sarah and her husband Moishe were also residing in Breslau and snuck out with them. In late October 1945, over four hours later, the small group arrived in Berlin. Eta's life as a communist party administrator was now over.

They all soon settled into an apartment in the Soviet sector of the city. Berlin was a city divided up among the Allies of World War II. But the Cold War was now under way, and the split of Berlin and Germany itself into two separate entities, one Communist and one Democratic, was to happen in the not too distant future. A chance visit one morning from a Soviet officer turned out to be a stroke of good fortune. He happened to be a Russian Jew who was seeking to purchase some Jewish prayer items, which Heniek and Moishe could get for him. When he saw Eta with her baby son, he knew he could trust them.

This officer had information that the Soviet authorities were soon going to close the border, sealing off the Soviet sector from the rest of the portions of Berlin. When he came back a few days later to pick up his holy items, everyone piled into his car. He drove them to Checkpoint Charlie at the Bradenburg Gate and across into the American sector. He dropped them off there and returned back to duty in the Soviet zone, which soon became East Berlin.

Shortly thereafter, they made their way to a displaced persons' camp and later into the town of Lapterheim, Germany, a suburb of Frankfurt. General Dwight Eisenhower had ordered the German residents of this town to leave their homes. The Wrobel family became part of the 1,000 Jews allowed to move into these homes. Heniek's sister, Sarah, and brother-in-law, Moishe, joined them. With World War II over and the horrific tragedy of the Holocaust now known to the world, some of the democratic nations including the United States, were now opening up to the idea of helping resettle refugees. The chance to move to the United States and make a life there was appealing to Eta and Heniek and to Sarah and Moishe too. They filed applications to come to the United States, and then they waited.

In the meantime, Heniek and Eta's baby son Hershel was a sickly child. Around the time he hit six months old, he contracted a form of rheumatic fever. They were able to get him into a German hospital. But the only doctor around who could best treat this disease happened to be a former Nazi doctor who spent the war working in the concentration camps. What this doctor could and would do now is what mattered most to Eta. Fortunately, the doctor came through. successfully treating Hershel and helping him recover to full health.

Shortly after taking her baby boy to the hospital for treatment, Eta had a visitor call upon her there. He was a British Army officer, a Jewish one at that. His name was Philip Gontarsky, Eta's first cousin. Philip was the son of Eta's Aunt Gitel, her mother's older sister. As newlyweds, long before World War II came to Poland, Gitel and her husband Benjamin had moved to England and made a life there.

Stationed in Germany since the war ended, Philip had been searching the displaced persons (DP) camps and interacting with the International Red Cross in hopes of finding his relatives he knew were from Poland, wondering if any survived. Eventually he located his first cousin Eta, whom he had never met before.

For Eta, connecting with her cousin at this time brought much joy. She was relieved to know that her Aunt Gitel was still alive and well and that Philip also had an older sister named Ettie. Philip let the hospital staff know that Eta and her baby boy should receive nothing but the best treatment. They were in good hands for the rest of their stay there.

In 1947, permission came from the American government that the Wrobels were all approved to move to the United States. There was great joy and anticipation for the new destination ahead. At the same time, they still had to wait as to when they would be allowed to board a ship to make this big move. Eta did not sit idly by. She was able to find a tutor to help her start learning English. She caught on quickly.

However, before the actual move took place, both joy and tragedy hit Eta and Heniek. The joy occurred on April 15, 1947 as a second child was born to Henry and Eta, a baby girl named Shaindel Rivka—named for each of their mothers.

The tragedy and great sorrow occurred a little later on. One evening Sarah, now pregnant, and Moishe were returning from attending a soccer match. They were riding in the back seat of a car with other people when the driver, attempting to pass a slow-moving vehicle in front of him, pulled out of the lane and was hit head-on by an oncoming truck. Moishe seeing the truck coming pushed Sarah out of the car in time. He and all the rest of the passengers in the car died from the crash, and Sarah lost their baby. Eta and Heniek were deeply saddened by the tragic accident that had come to Sarah and her family. They would keep Sarah close by them for a while.

Then the official news came that they could depart Europe. On August 6, 1947, Eta and Heniek with their two small children, along with Sarah, were able to board a ship and set sail for America. Nine days later they arrived in New York City—immigrants ready and anxious to start a new life.

$\mathcal{E}$pilogue

The story of Eta and Heniek Wrobel's life in the United States after coming to this country in mid-August 1947 is the classic story of how immigrants have made such significant and positive contributions to American history. With little money in their possession when they arrived, they worked hard, raised a family with solid values and a good education, and especially in Eta's case, made service part of their lives. They were the rags-to-riches story of newcomers who were determined to make a positive difference.

They stayed in New York City upon landing in America, living over the years in three of the city's boroughs—the Bronx, Brooklyn, and Manhattan. Their third child, a daughter named Anna Miriam, was born in Brooklyn on July 25, 1950. Heniek Wrobel, forever after going by the name of Henry Wrobel, got started by running small grocery or corner market stores, bodegas as New Yorkers call these stores, in those initial years in New York. Eta worked right alongside him helping run the stores as they moved from one location to another over time while raising their three children.

As the Wrobels carefully saved their money one dollar at a time, Henry bought into a real estate development business. His business hit at the right time, building many of the homes for the borough of Staten Island. As the decade of the 1960s progressed, Henry and Eta experienced a fair amount of financial success.

They would enjoy the success from the fruits of their labor for the rest of their lives.

As Eta no longer needed to work with Henry, she spent her time volunteering in many service organizations. Not surprisingly, she usually took on leadership roles in these endeavors. The service organizations she was most devoted to were ones focused on supporting the welfare and development of the nation of Israel. The women's organization Hadassah and Israel Bonds were two of the prime examples of this.

Nothing pleased Eta more than seeing the return of a homeland for the Jewish people through the establishment and growth of the state of Israel. In the case of Hadassah, chapters for this service organization throughout North America are typically based around geographic location. In Eta's case, she started her own Hadassah chapter with members coming from around the greater New York City area, not a particular vicinity. The commonalty among the members who joined this chapter was that they were all Holocaust survivors. Eta created a safe environment for these women to come together and to not have to worry how they expressed themselves since none were native English speakers. The chapter, of course, did very well under Eta's leadership, successfully raising funds to support services in Israel.

Another example, among many, of Eta's skills in outstanding leadership and commitment to service was AKIM. This organization, which was started in 1951, provides educational, vocational, and other support services for people with intellectual and developmental disabilities in Israel.

Around 1981, the director of AKIM approached Eta asking for her help to set up a fundraising support organization in the United States. She hesitated about getting involved. She knew Henry's concerns about her spreading herself too thin and then not being around to spend quality time with family. But she was touched by the good work AKIM was doing during her visit to one of its centers for handicapped children in Tel Aviv. Then, upon hearing Henry's blessings—why would you say no to helping such a good cause was his message—Eta went forward and Friends of AKIM USA was launched. Under Eta's leadership, the United States support organization set up chapters around the country, and over the years raised millions in funds for AKIM's important work in Israel.

Here is how Eta's daughter, Shain, described her mother to an audience honoring Eta at a Friends of AKIM fundraising event on its 13th anniversary: "My mother, throughout her life, views herself as a soldier, fighting for her survival, the survival of her family, and the survival of Israel. Like an officer in the Israeli army, as she does in leading AKIM, she leads by saying follow me."

Today Shain's reflections about her mother still speak about Eta's great talent for leadership. She did not lead by being a dictator. Instead, she built relationships, was a strong organizer, and reached out to people to seek their involvement—especially their money to support the cause. With her positive and assertive manner, people did not want to say no to Eta when she came asking for something.

In fact, spending time in Israel became a vital part of Eta and Henry's life. As their three children grew up and went off on their own, along with achieving a sense of economic well-being, Henry and Eta frequently travelled to Israel over the years. Eta's service work in these Jewish organizations—in support of Israel—had her, on occasion, meeting with prominent Israeli government leaders, such as Yitzhak Rabin, Shimon Peres, and Ariel Sharon, who all served as prime ministers.

These trips to Israel also found Henry and Eta greatly enjoying the country and spending time with family and friends who lived there. Their oldest child Hershel, known as Hal as an adult, went for six months to volunteer in Israel at the age of 28. He ultimately stayed and made his life there. Seeing Hal and the family he would have, was a major part of the joy of these visits.

Henry also had family who settled in Israel whom they would also visit. Eta took Liza Melnick, the daughter of one of Henry's cousins, under her wing when Liza was a teen. Liza would eventually feel like a fourth child to her. Liza was 14 when her mother died. Eta and Henry stepped in to help pay for her education and welcomed Liza into their home on numerous visits to New York. Liza has now raised her own family, and has had a fine career in special education, remaining close to Eta and Henry throughout the rest of their lives.

In addition, visits with many friends living in Israel kept these trips busy and enjoyable too. One of the friends they would see was Moshe Danyilak, one of Eta's fellow partisans in her unit who made his life in Israel after the war. The young man she met and befriended during her role as mayor of Lukow, Yankel Kesselbrenner, was also among the friends they looked in on each time they made trips to Israel.

Early on when they arrived in New York City in the late 1940s, Henry and Eta attended gatherings of the Lukower Society. This was a social organization of Polish Jews who originally came from Lukow, Poland, Eta's original home town. Eta and Henry were welcomed from the start. Eta enjoyed meeting a few Lukow-origin people who knew either her mother or father in their younger years. These folks were lucky enough to immigrate to the United States prior to the Holocaust years. Hearing them share their pleasant memories of her beloved parents brought Eta some comfort.

Many of the friends Eta and Henry socialized with in New York had something in common with them besides being immigrants. They were Holocaust survivors too. In fact, among the couples the Wrobels would see periodically, who also resided in

New York City, were Jack (formerly Yidl) Woland and his wife Lola, a Holocaust survivor from the concentration camps, as well as Hyman (formerly Chaim) Grinbaum and his wife Chana, also a Holocaust survivor. One of the early places the Wrobel family settled in New York was in a Bronx apartment building where the Woland family also resided. The Wolands raised two sons there. Jack Woland worked as a butcher and lived a full life, passing away at the age of 89.

Hyman Grinbaum who met his wife in a displaced persons' camp in Italy raised two daughters and two sons, had a fine career as a tailor, and lived until the age of 95. In fact, late in life on a visit with his son Jay to the U.S. Holocaust Memorial Museum in Washington, D.C., Hyman went into a cattle car replica there and started climbing up to the top of it to show his son how he escaped to get into the woods. Even as an old man, he remained quite strong.

Hyman maintained contact over the years with another key member of the partisan unit, David Rendel. He too married a Holocaust survivor, Molly, who was a second cousin of his. She survived the war in Poland, living under a false Christian identity the whole time. David and his wife Molly made their lives in the Los Angeles area and had one daughter and one son. David ran a television and radio repair business and later a furniture store. Molly worked along side him as the bookkeeper in these businesses. They both lived full lives, David passing away at the age of 93 and Molly at the age of 91.

For Eta, certain values, such as equality and respect for all, that she was raised with never left her. In particular, she was greatly bothered by acts of intolerance and discrimination and was one who tended to speak her mind if she saw people mistreated.

The story of the bus ride in London was just one example of many. She greatly admired Martin Luther King, Jr. and his civil rights movement and was saddened by his murder in April of 1968. By the 1980s, this sense of social justice sparked Eta to start speaking in public events and in schools about the Holocaust and her experience in it. She wanted this horrible tragedy to be understood and remembered so as not to ever be repeated or denied. After all, she had withstood and emerged from this tragedy with no parents and as the only one of ten children who survived. She would summarize her partisan experience saying that the best way she resisted the Nazis "was to survive."

But Eta did more than survive, she thrived in her life. After the initial years and struggles as an immigrant trying to make it in her new world of the United States, this once very serious woman, her adult children noticed, started to grow in her zest for life. Her daughter Anna remarked, "It was as if my mother was living for all her family who did not get a chance for a full life." Her sense of humor began to show much more than in the early years. She would tell jokes and had a great laugh too. Well into her forties and fifties, sometimes when Eta came by a park and saw a pickup game of soccer going on, she would jump in and play for a bit. Her great athleticism even at that age showed, as she held her own in these games.

In addition, on at least three occasions, Eta received invitations to a family's wedding or bar or bat mitzvah without being familiar with whom the inviting party was. Since the events were in the New York City vicinity, she decided to go with Henry. The same thing happened each time. The person behind the invitation was someone who had been saved by the rescue network Eta had created in her resistance role in the villages of eastern Poland. At these events, time would be taken to acknowledge and recognize Eta for her heroic efforts, which was always quite a pleasant surprise.

Eta passed away on May 26, 2008 at the age of 92. A heart surgery Eta felt she needed, which her family wished she would not go through with at the time, was responsible for her death although not immediately. She spent her last six months living near her daughter, Shain, in upstate New York to get regular care after the procedure. But she never recovered from it. Henry lived on for nearly five more years, passing away on March 10, 2013, at the age of 94.

Beyond the leadership and service this woman of valor demonstrated throughout her life and the qualities of intelligence, courage, and compassion people often used to describe her, a big part of Eta's legacy was family. Eta grew up in a close-knit family and instilled a strong sense of family in her three children.

Although they have been far apart geographically, Anna, who lives outside of Portland, Maine, Shain, who lives two hours north of New York City, and Hal, who lived in Israel. (Sadly, Hal passed away suddenly on November 9, 2018. He was found alone in his home slumped down in his chair, the victim of an apparent heart attack or stroke.), they regularly kept in touch with each other over the years and remained close. The special occasions that brought them together along with their children have always been joyous gatherings. Between Anna, Shain, and Hal, they gave Eta and Henry eight grandchildren, and they each have grandchildren themselves today.

One of Eta's grandsons is Barak Wrobel, the son of Anna Wrobel. He currently serves on the board of the Jewish Partisan Educational Foundation. It is an organization that provides vital materials about Jewish resistance fighters during the Holocaust to teachers and educational organizations.

Barak's mother divorced not long after he was born, so he and his older sister Corinna grew up in a single-parent household. Still, he feels very fortunate that he grew up in New York City because living close by and playing an active role in his life were his grandparents, Henry and Eta.

Barak is the first person I met from the Wrobel family when exploring the idea of writing this book about his grandmother's partisan experience. He not only encouraged me to go forward, saying his family would support this effort (which proved to be very true), but he also shared memories of his grandmother, Eta, that remain so vibrant years later.

As he stated, "She was a strong and dynamic presence who made such a positive impact on so many people." This statement sums up well who this woman of valor was—Eta Chait, Jewish resistance leader.

$\mathcal{B}$ibliography

Books

Bachrach, Susan and Kassof, Anita. *Flight and Rescue.* Washington, D.C.: U.S. Holocaust Memorial Museum, 2001.

Czubaszek, Krzystztof. *The Jews of Lukow and Vicinity.* Danmar: Warsaw, Poland, 2008.

Heller, Celia S. *On the Edge of Destruction: Jews of Poland Between Two World Wars.* New York: Columbia University Press, 1977.

Hoffman, Eva. Shtetl, *The Life and Death of a Small Town and the World of Polish Jews.* Boston: Houghton Mifflin Company, 1997.

Miron, Guy and Shulhani, Shlomit, Editors. *The Yad Vashem Encyclopedia of the Ghettos During the Holocaust.* Jerusalem, Israel: Yad Vashem, The Holocaust Martyrs' and Heroes' Remembrance Authority, 2009.

Paldiel, Mordecai. *Saving the Jews: Amazing Stories of Men and Women Who Defied the"Final Solution."* Schreiber Publishing: Rockville, MD, 2000.

Tec, Nechoma. *When Light Pierced Darkness: Christian Rescue of Jews in Nazi-Occupied Poland.* Oxford University Press: New York, 1986.

Werner, Harold. *Fighting Back: A Memoir of Jewish Resistance in World War II.* Columbia University Press: New York, 1992.

Wrobel, Eta with Friedman, Jeanette. *My Life My Way: The extraordinary memoir of a Jewish Partisan in WWII Poland.* The Wordsmithy, LLC: New Milford, NJ, 2006.

Video Sources

PBS Documentary, 2002: *Resistance: Untold Stories of Jewish Partisans.* Jewish Partisan Educational Foundation video clips on Eta Wrobel Shoah Foundation videos:

- Eta Wrobel
- Molly Rendel
- Manny Orlinsky

About the Author

Marty Brounstein is an accomplished storyteller and author who has been on a journey sharing a true stories of courage, compassion, and rescue from the Holocaust. His first book in the area, also produced by Square One Publishers, is *The Righteous Few: Two Who Made a Difference*. Over the years, with this book, Marty has delivered storytelling presentations to a wide variety of audiences and multiple cities around the U.S. about its two unsung heroes, Frans and Hermina Wijnakker, a Dutch Christian couple that saved the lives of more than two dozen Jews during the Holocaust.

These storytelling events have been held in churches, synagogues, Muslim-based organizations, a multitude of service organizations, bookstores, libraries, private homes, schools, colleges, book clubs, Jewish Community Centers, and history and Holocaust museums. He has also facilitated book discussions inside many school classrooms and had insightful discussions with book clubs. He has built a workshop using the power of this story and the theme of making a positive difference that he has taken into numerous workplaces and professional conferences. Titled "The Courage and Compassion to Do the Right Thing: A Lesson in Making a Positive Difference," the workshop focuses on the inspirational value of this story and its positive messages and lessons so relevant for our lives today.

On this journey, Marty has been studying others involved in resistance and rescue in the Holocaust—Jews and non-Jews alike—and has been delivering presentations about them titled "Heroes of the Holocaust." The stories he tells are of these unsung and often unknown heroes.

Marty received his BA degree in Education and History from National College of Education in Evanston, IL and his Masters in Industrial Relations from the University of Oregon in Eugene, OR. Early in his career Marty was an educator who taught history, including on the Holocaust. After a stint as a human resources executive, Marty then ran a management consulting business for more than twenty-five years, specializing in leadership and organizational development with clients across many industries.

Through this work, he has been the author or contributing author for eight books related to business management, including *Coaching and Mentoring For Dummies, Communicating Effectively For Dummies,* and *Managing Teams For Dummies.* The stories he now writes about tell of the unsung and often unknown heroes of the Holocaust. His latest and second book with Square One Publishers is *Woman of Valor,* which focuses on a Jewish woman resistance leader in the woods of Poland during the Holocaust.

For his service with his book, *The Righteous Few: Two Who Made a Difference,* over the years, in the fall of 2019 Marty became a recipient of the Jefferson Award out of the San Francisco Bay Area region. This award comes from an organization now called Multiplying Good, originally founded in 1972 by among others Jacqueline Kennedy Onassis. It recognizes people who perform acts of service and public good for America.

Currently, Marty resides in San Mateo, California with his wife, Leah Baars. To learn more about Marty's speaking engagements and workshops, please visit www.MartyABrounstein.com

Other Square One Titles of Interest

The Righteous Few

Two Who Made a Difference

Marty Brounstein

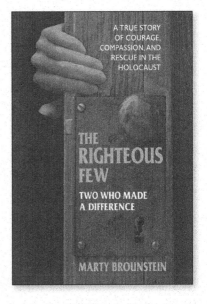

The Righteous Few is a remarkable true tale of courage, compassion, and rescue during the Holocaust. It is the story of a young married Christian couple, Frans and Mien Wijnakker, living in the Netherlands during World War II. When their country was under the brutal occupation of Nazi Germany, they got involved, when most did not, in the risky and dangerous work of helping the people most in need. By the end of the war, they had managed to save more than two dozen Jews from certain death. Their heroism later earned them a special recognition of "Righteous Among the Nations" by Yad Vashem, the World Holocaust Remembrance Center.

Frans and Mien were Catholics who led a simple life in the countryside of southeastern Holland. They had four small children of their own. But a simple *yes* in response to a call for help during a business trip to Amsterdam profoundly changed Frans' and his wife's lives. In a two-year period, they took many Jewish refugees into their own home and organized a rescue network that placed refugees in other people's homes, as well. As their rescue work increased, so did the many risks and dangers associated with it. They faced one of their most difficult challenges when they took in a young pregnant Jewish woman and her husband. How do you help someone who has to give birth in hiding? Through this and many other stories, *The Righteous Few* draws a vivid picture of two extraordinary people who shined the light of hope during one of history's darkest periods.

$16.95 US • 186 pages • 6 x 9-inch paperback • ISBN 978-0-7570-0497-1

The Defiant

A True Story of Escape, Survival & Resistance

Shalom Yoran

Fifty years ago, while recuperating in an Israeli hospital, a young Polish refugee wrote at length about his remarkable experiences in war-torn Europe. When done, his notes were set aside as he built a new life for himself, his wife, and their children. Then, in 1995, Shalom Yoran came across his own long-forgotten writings and, realizing their importance, completed his work. *The Defiant* is his extraordinary memoir.

The Defiant is a true story of survival and courage in the darkest days of Nazi-occupied Poland. It is the personal account of a young man who refused to yield to the German onslaught, and instead chose to become a Jewish resistance fighter. The book chronicles the bravery of a small group of determined men and women who carried on a forest war, using antiquated guns and living on instinct. From the brutal behavior of Polish peasants to the constant bombardment of German air raids, from the questionable orders of anti-Semitic commanders to direct confrontations with storm troopers, the author sheds light on events that few know of in this country.

Yoran has written a unique holocaust account that is fresh, powerful, and rich in detail. Here is the amazing story of a handful of courageous men and women who fought against incredible odds—and triumphed.

$15.95 US • 304 pages • 6 x 9-inch paperback • ISBN 978-0-7570-0078-2

L'Chaim!

Pictures to Evoke
Memories of Jewish Life

Eliezer Sobel

"I think this is a great idea and it would be very useful, indeed. I never really thought about it, but it makes a lot of sense. I fully support and endorse the concept."

–Rudolph E. Tanzi, Ph.D., Professor of Neurology at Harvard University Medical School

In spending time with his mother in the advanced stages of Alzheimer's disease, Eliezer Sobel recognized something astounding: Although she had seemingly lost all of her language skills several years earlier, she still enjoyed gazing at pictures in magazines, and she actually read the headlines aloud! He searched for a simple picture book with easy-to-read captions in big print, but learned that while there are over twenty thousand books designed for caregivers, there are virtually no books written for patients with dementia.

L'Chaim: Pictures to Evoke Memories of Jewish Life was created specifically for Jewish elders who suffer from some form of memory loss. Pictures and captions stimulate the recollection of past events and provide tender moments of connection between caregivers and loved ones.

$17.95 US • 32 pages • 11 x 8.5-inch hardback • ISBN 978-1-937907-44-0

The King of Shabbos

And Other Stories of Return

Zalman Velvel

How often do you read a story that makes you laugh out loud or wipe tears from your eyes? It's rare to find honest writing that is powerful, moving, and inspirational, but words that come from the heart enter the heart. From the voice of a man who has struggled, hurt, and grown—and laughed with joy over the process—comes *The King of Shabbos and Other Stories of Return,* a collection of eighteen tales that will make you think and feel in a new and different way.

Zalman Velvel is simply a storyteller. As you read his tales, you will come to intimately know his characters, some of whom you may recognize from your own life, and some of whom may even remind you of yourself. You will grieve with them in their sorrows, and feel joy as they experience spiritual awakening. And regardless of your age, background, or circumstances, your life will be the richer for having met them.

The inspirational theme that runs throughout these tales, tying them together, is the idea of returning to simple Jewish values and spiritual meaning in a world where values and meanings get traded and lost. Many of Zalman's stories won awards when they first appeared in publications around the world, but here, for the first time, is a single volume of his most poignant work. Truly, Zalman's characters and their stories will become a part of you. They may even teach you a lesson or two about love, life, and lasting meaning.

$24.95 US • 224 pages • 6 x 9-inch paperback • ISBN 978-0-7570-0246-5